PILLARS
TO FINDING YOUR
PURPOSE

A HANDBOOK FOR MAKING THE MOST OF YOUR LIFE

TERRY GOGNA

10 Pillars to Finding Your Purpose
By Terry Gogna

Copyright © 2024 Terry Gogna
ISBN: 9798342032360

Edited by Anil Gogna, Aaron Gogna and Ricky Verma

Published by Terry Gogna Inc.
www.TerryGogna.com

Dedication

This book is dedicated to my newborn granddaughter, my precious Nilaya. Your arrival has filled my heart with renewed purpose and joy. Every time I look into your beautiful eyes, I am inspired to stay healthy and strong so we can share countless adventures together in the years to come.

As you grow, may God's love continually guide and protect you, showering you with joy, laughter, and adventure. As we surround you with endless love, may you always find the courage to pursue your passions and uncover your purpose early in life, filling your heart with meaning as you make a lasting impact on your family and the world.

This book is a testament to the love and inspiration you've already brought into my life, even though it's only been one month.

Love you always,
Papa

Table of Contents

Introduction

Why is it that people are willing to spend countless hours planning a vacation, yet not take any significant time to plan their life, or, more importantly, discover their purpose? For me, the truth was simple: I didn't know how to discover my life's purpose.

The aim of this book is to broaden your perspective beyond your current viewpoint. Remember what Captain Kirk said, "Space: the final frontier. These are the voyages of the starship Enterprise. Its five-year mission: to explore strange new worlds, to seek out new life and new civilizations, to boldly go where no one has gone before." Even though this is an incredible mission statement, most of us are not going on a space journey anytime soon. So, maybe this will relate better:

"Life: the ultimate frontier. These are the journeys of individuals seeking purpose. Their mission: to venture into uncharted territories, unearth their true purpose, and fearlessly embrace a future full of boundless opportunities."

As we turn the pages of this book, join me in embracing

challenges, uncovering hidden truths, and crafting a future that is full of passion and fulfillment—your life's purpose.

Foundation:
Purpose Through Education

"Education is the most powerful weapon which you can use to change the world."

- Nelson Mandela

From the moment we step into school as children, we embark on a journey filled with learning, exploration, and discovery. Education isn't just about books and exams; it's a rich tapestry woven with experiences that shape who we are and what we aspire to become. Through a diverse curriculum that includes academics, sports, and special activities, school offers us the chance to learn about the world and ourselves.

The Role of Parents in Broadening Experiences

Beyond the school environment, parents play a crucial role in exposing their children to activities that broaden their life experiences. Encouraging involvement in community service, sports, arts, and cultural events can significantly enhance a child's education. These experiences offer real-world lessons that classrooms alone cannot provide. When parents introduce their children to various activities, they cultivate curiosity and a willingness to explore. This exposure helps children discover interests and talents they might not encounter within the confines of a traditional educational setting.

Engaging in diverse experiences fosters adaptability and social skills, enabling children to navigate different environments and build relationships with a variety of people. Additionally, parents model the importance of lifelong learning. By participating in activities alongside their children or supporting their endeavors, they demonstrate that exploration and growth are essential aspects of life. This encourages a mindset where children feel empowered to seek out new opportunities, both inside and outside the classroom.

The Role of Education in Self-Discovery

As we navigate our school years, we're encouraged to explore a variety of activities that can help us uncover our talents and interests. In the classroom, we encounter a wide array of subjects—math, science, literature, and the arts. Each subject opens a door to new ideas and perspectives, encouraging curiosity and critical thinking. However, learning doesn't stop at academics. Participation in sports, music, drama, and clubs provides invaluable opportunities to explore interests beyond the traditional curriculum.

These activities teach us essential life skills: teamwork, discipline, and resilience. They also help us identify our unique abilities and passions. Whether it's the thrill of scoring a goal in soccer, the joy of performing on stage, or the satisfaction of creating art, these experiences guide us toward understanding what resonates with us. These formative years serve as a foundation for the future, helping us realize our potential and leading us closer to our true passions.

The Importance of Higher Education

Now, when it comes time to consider higher education, many students face the dilemma of whether to pursue a degree or chase their passion right away. The purpose of going to university extends beyond obtaining a diploma; it is about gaining further exposure and depth in areas of interest. University allows us to delve deeper into subjects we are passionate about while continuing to develop essential skills that are valuable in any field.

For some, pursuing a degree may serve as a safety net. It provides not only a backup plan for financial stability but also the opportunity to refine skills that can enhance our pursuit of passion. Education equips us with critical thinking, problem-solving, and communication skills— tools that are invaluable no matter the career path we choose.

Access to Learning in the Digital Age

Moreover, we live in an age where knowledge is at our fingertips. Through books and social media videos, we can literally learn about anything. We can explore all facets of the world and broaden our horizons in every field of education. Online platforms provide access to a wealth of information, allowing us to discover new interests, learn new skills, and gain insights from diverse perspectives. I encourage you to learn more through these resources rather than just using them for entertainment purposes. This abundance of resources empowers us to supplement our formal education and dive deeper into topics that ignite our passions.

If You're Unsure of Your Path

What if you're uncertain about your future? This is where the structure of university or college becomes a significant advantage. It offers an environment conducive to self-discovery and growth, allowing you time to reflect on your interests and values while gaining qualifications. Even if you're unsure of your direction, attending university can help clarify your goals and passions.

Think of your degree as an investment in your future. It may not seem directly related to your ultimate career path, but the knowledge and skills acquired during this time can open doors you never anticipated. Life is unpredictable, and having a degree can provide you with more options when navigating the complexities of your career.

Playing Your Cards Right

In this journey, my advice is to play your cards right. Pursuing a degree can give you a strategic advantage, even if your initial interests seem unrelated to your studies. The world is full of examples of individuals who used their education as a springboard to achieve their dreams, often in fields that initially seemed distant from their academic background.

Once you've secured that foundation, you can fully commit to your passion without the pressure of financial uncertainty. You'll be empowered to explore creative pursuits, start your own ventures, or engage in meaningful community work, all while knowing you have a solid backup plan.

Conclusion

Ultimately, the decision between attending university and pursuing your passion doesn't have to be a binary choice. Education can serve as the launchpad for your journey, providing you with the experiences, skills, and safety net needed to find your true calling. Embrace the journey of self-discovery, and remember that finding your purpose is often a winding path filled with exploration, growth, and unexpected revelations. Whether you choose to attend university or dive straight into your passion, the key is to remain open to possibilities and committed to the journey ahead.

PILLAR 1: What is a Purpose?

"A purpose is like a cause that never ends; it could never be fully accomplished. It could only continuously change lives for the better."

- Victor Frankl

Before delving into the definition of purpose, let's clarify some commonly confused terms and highlight their distinct meanings.

PASSION: Something we love doing—an activity that sparks enthusiasm and brings joy to our lives. It's characterized by a genuine and intense interest, dedication, and emotional investment.

DREAM: A strongly desired goal, something we passionately want to achieve or experience—the fuel that propels us to act.

VISION: A clear and inspiring mental image of what we want to achieve in the future—a well-defined idea of our goals, values, and the path we want to take in life.

MISSION: Encompasses the actions an individual or organization takes to achieve its goals and fulfill its purpose. It's the practical roadmap for realizing our vision.

GOAL: A specific, measurable result we aim to accomplish within a defined time frame. It provides a clear target for our efforts.

PURPOSE: In the book, 'Man's Search for Meaning,' Victor Frankl defines purpose as, **"Purpose in your life is not success, money or fame. Those are goals; purpose is something greater, it's like a cause that never ends and can never be fully accomplished. It can only continuously change lives for the better."**

Our purpose is the power behind our dreams, the true WHY, which ultimately determines their realization. It's the reason we want to achieve a specific dream. Our purpose gives meaning to our life; it's aligned with our values, drives us to act and shapes the way we live.

Our purpose is the foundation of our goals, vision, mission, and dream. Without a purpose, nothing will happen.

"If we have a dream to be the best or to reach the highest level in our field, without a purpose we won't be able to endure the struggles that come with it" —Sun Myung Moon.

If we find ourselves saying, "I've found my dream!", yet struggle to maintain consistent effort, it may be necessary to reassess or rediscover our purpose.

Terry Gogna

The GREATNESS of a person is shaped by their purpose and the sacrifices they make. The higher the purpose, the greater the sacrifices required to accomplish it.

A higher purpose generally helps a larger number of people and addresses more significant, collective issues, as seen in the role of a community leader (such as an activist fighting for a specific cause, a politician working on social justice policies, a nonprofit director managing disaster relief efforts, or a religious/spiritual leader guiding a congregation through moral or ethical challenges). In contrast, a lower purpose tends to impact fewer individuals and focuses on more immediate, personal goals, such as those of a mom or dad (providing individual emotional support during challenging times, mentoring children, or creating a stable home environment). However, it's important to recognize that the purpose of a mom or dad, while more localized, is profoundly significant. The care and support provided within a family are invaluable and have a lasting impact on the lives of their children, who will grow up to be great leaders and contributors to the community of the next generation.

PILLAR 2: Why Having a Purpose Matters

"A purpose gives meaning to our life, inspires us to act, and fills our heart with joy"

- Terry Gogna

Research studies published in the Journal of Positive Psychology, Journal of Substance Abuse Treatment, Journal of Clinical Psychology, and from institutions like the University of California, Berkeley, the University of Pennsylvania, and the Harvard School of Public Health have shown that:

People with a defined sense of purpose in life:

1. Tend to have a sense of direction, meaning, and fulfillment, which helps them stay focused and motivated even when faced with challenges.

Having a clear sense of direction and meaning gives individuals an internal compass that keeps them grounded and focused, even during difficult times. When challenges arise, instead of feeling lost or overwhelmed, they view obstacles as opportunities to grow and learn. Their purpose acts as a stabilizing force, helping them stay motivated and resilient. With a strong sense of fulfillment, they are less likely to be swayed by temporary setbacks, knowing that each step, whether forward or backward, brings them closer to their ultimate goal.

2. Tend to have a higher self-esteem and confidence.

This inner strength manifests not only in their mindset but also in their physical presence. They tend to walk with purpose, upright and assured, rarely slouching or appearing uncertain. Their determined posture signals to others that they are on a clear path, and, as a result, people often step aside, allowing them to move forward unhindered on their journey.

3. Tend to use their purpose as a guide to make better decisions.

They often describe their purpose as a 'North Star'—a constant, guiding force that keeps them on course. No matter how difficult or unpredictable life becomes, their North Star remains in sight, providing clarity and ensuring they stay aligned with their deeper goals and values, as well as with what gives them meaning in their life.

Throughout history, even great spiritual figures like Jesus and many saints sought solitude on mountaintops to gain clarity and reconnect with their purpose. By physically rising above the noise and distractions of the world below, they were able to focus more intently on their mission and deepen their connection to their spiritual calling. This symbolic act of ascending to higher ground reflects the universal human desire to elevate one's perspective in order to see more clearly and realign with one's true purpose. Just as they sought these moments of reflection, individuals today can benefit from stepping back from daily pressures to reconnect with their own 'North Star.'"

4. Tend to have an increased level of mental and emotional well-being, as well as greater overall satisfaction and success in life.

When you feel good about yourself, this sense of well-being often translates into action. Confidence and self-assurance fuel a desire to strive for higher goals, push past limitations, and achieve more. As a result, people with a strong sense of purpose tend to seek opportunities for growth, take on new challenges, and actively contribute to the world around them.

5. Surprisingly, they also tend to have a better immune system and lower levels of inflammation, which may contribute to longer and healthier lives.

This connection between purpose and physical health may stem from the reduced stress and increased mental well-being that come with having a clear sense of direction. People who feel purposeful often experience lower levels of anxiety and depression, which are known to negatively affect the immune system. By maintaining a positive outlook and engaging in meaningful activities, they not only nurture their mental and emotional health but also foster better overall physical well-being, leading to a more balanced and healthier life.

PILLAR 3: Consequence of Living Without a Purpose

"The absence of purpose is like sailing without a compass; drifting aimlessly to an unfulfilled life."

- Terry Gogna

Research studies have shown that people who live without a clear sense of purpose often struggle with a lack of motivation, boredom, and loneliness. This can lead to chronic stress, which increases the risk of both physical and mental health problems. Without direction, some may turn to excessive drinking, drug use, or even engage in criminal activities. In extreme cases, the absence of purpose can contribute to family breakdowns and depression.

You must be aware: if you continue on your current path without making any changes, where will your life end up? Are you looking forward to that destination? Because, if nothing changes, you'll be there soon.

Living life as it comes, without purpose, is like being on a boat with no sails, no oars, and no motor—adrift on the open ocean. With nothing to guide or drive us forward, **we're left at the mercy of the elements: the wind, rain, and waves shaping our fate.** Powerless and feeling like spectators in our own lives, we can only wait to see

where life will take us, uncertain whether it will bring fortune or hardship.

MAYBE ONE DAY we'll wake to **dolphins** swimming gracefully beside us, thinking, 'How lucky I am to witness this beauty.' But the truth is, we didn't create this moment—it happened by chance. And while this time it brought joy, there's no guarantee the next twist of fate will be as kind.

MAYBE ONE DAY, we'll wake up to the realization that, despite thinking we were making progress—feeling the gentle rocking of the waves beneath our boat—five years have passed, and we're still in the same place we started. We've been **drifting in circles**, and the only thing that's changed is our age. What a waste of life. Nothing else has shifted: we're still in the same job, with the same income, the same lifestyle, the same debt, and the same struggles. Our hopes remain, but without action, they've led us nowhere.

MAYBE ONE DAY, we'll wake to find that strong winds have smashed our boat **into the rocks**. These rocks symbolize the tragedies and mistakes that could have been avoided if we had taken action instead of procrastinating—like accumulating massive debt, falling into drug addiction out of boredom, mental illness brought on by stress, a broken family strained by the pressures of life or a sudden serious health challenge due to neglect. Without preparation, self-reflection, or the desire to change our ways, we were left vulnerable to disaster.

Maybe one day, we'll find ourselves **shipwrecked** on a desert island. At first, it may seem like paradise—palm trees, coconuts, bananas, and beaches—but soon, we'll realize it's not what we thought. We didn't choose to be here; we're in the wrong place. This island symbolizes being stuck in the wrong job, the wrong career, the wrong relationship, the wrong neighborhood, the wrong house—leaving us feeling completely lost and stranded. Without purpose or direction, we end up in situations that don't align with our true desires, isolated and unsure of how we got here, trapped in a life we never intended to live.

Maybe one day, we see a hurricane on the horizon but choose to ignore it, thinking it won't impact our boat or our life. As the wind changes direction, **the hurricane** brings 50-foot waves crashing down upon us, flipping the boat upside down and plunging it into the dark ocean. This symbolizes the devastation of losing a job unexpectedly, facing a serious health challenge due to neglect, the end of a significant relationship due to stress, or massive financial problems. It turns our world upside down, leaving us overwhelmed and struggling to find our way amidst the wreckage. We saw the storm approaching but chose to ignore the warning signs. Instead of taking action, we relied solely on positive thinking, hoping it would be enough to prevent the disaster. What an avoidable tragedy.

So, what's the message here? We need to stop drifting aimlessly in our boat. It's time to take hold of the oars, raise the sails, or even attach a motor, and start steering our life in a direction that aligns with our desires and brings us fulfillment. We need to find that purpose. However, let's not fall into the trap of believing we can control every aspect of our journey. Instead, let's leave a little room—say, 5%—for the unexpected, trusting that God might have some better plans in store for us.

Ron had worked at the same company for 23 years, and at the age of 55, he was suddenly laid off. He was blindsided by the news; he never imagined it could happen to him. The shock left him devastated, plunging him into severe depression because his job was not just a role but his entire life. With no other passions or purpose, and without a family or other significant relationships, Ron felt utterly lost. His depression deepened to the point where he checked himself into a clinic due to suicidal thoughts. He often lamented, "I'm 55 going on 85," feeling he had nothing else to live for. He mistakenly regarded his job as his sole purpose, the only source of meaning in his life.

A true purpose provides meaning and value to our life, it is not something that can be taken away. A purpose is not a possession or a title but a "why"—the fundamental reason behind what we do.

PILLAR 4: Mindset for Discovering Your Purpose

"A fixed mindset limits potential; embrace growth, and discover your purpose."

- Anonymous

Purpose Chapters: In life, we all have one overarching, deep purpose that will ultimately define who we are. However, discovering that purpose isn't easy because before we arrive at it, we go through many "purpose chapters." These chapters are phases in our life where we chase a specific goal that, at the time, feels like our true purpose. But a purpose chapter only lasts for a season before it fades, making way for the next one. This constant shift happens because we grow and change. The key is to understand that each chapter equips us with the skills we need for the next. It's not just about acquiring new abilities, though—our mindset and heart also evolve, giving us greater confidence and a fresh perspective on life. Ultimately, we need to trust that each purpose chapter is leading us toward our true, ultimate purpose.

It's also crucial that we don't view the end of a chapter as a sign of failure or think we've made a mistake. Reaching the end of one purpose chapter is not an indication that we shouldn't try again. Rather, it's part of the natural process of growth and discovery. Every chapter, even when it closes, has served its role in preparing us for the next step in our journey.

Stay Committed: Finding our purpose in life can feel daunting and challenging for most people, but it's crucial not to give up, no matter how long the journey takes. Purpose isn't something that simply appears overnight; it demands **commitment**—an unwavering dedication that includes patience, perseverance, and self-discovery. It takes an incredible amount of effort to uncover what truly makes our heart sing. There will be times when the search feels pointless, when you may ask yourself, "Why am I doing this?" or "Will I ever find it?" During these moments of doubt, the most important thing is to keep going.

A bad plan is always better than no plan at all because it gets you moving forward, even if you're unsure of where exactly you're headed. As you dive deeper into the process, things will gradually become clearer. Each step, even if it feels insignificant at the time, brings you closer to understanding your true purpose. The key is to stay committed, trusting that every challenge, every wrong turn, and every moment of doubt is part of the journey.

Live with purpose 7 days a week: People have been conditioned to follow a flawed script: study, get a job, work until you're 65, and only then, after retirement, do you finally get to live your dream life. This way of thinking is absurd. We are meant to be living with passion and purpose throughout our entire lives, not postponing it for a distant future. Waiting for retirement to live fully is a disservice to ourselves.

Vacations shouldn't be the rare moments when we get to enjoy life. We should be living intentionally every single day, pursuing something meaningful that fuels our passion. Having a purpose isn't just about working toward a goal—it's about making every day count because you're striving for something that gives your life meaning.

Too many people endure the weekdays, living for the weekends, where they finally feel free to do what they love. They're essentially living only two days a week, while merely "getting through" the other five. This is a terrible way to live. If you have a purpose, you'll live seven days a week, pursuing it with everything you've got. Your life won't just be waiting for weekends or vacations—it will be a daily journey filled with passion and meaning.

Think Beyond Yourself: Selfish goals are often limited in their impact and duration. Once you achieve them, their significance can quickly wane, and when challenges arise, it's easy to abandon them. Take, for example, the pursuit of building a business with the goal of purchasing a luxury car. This is not a purpose; it's a goal or a dream. The pursuit ends once you acquire the car, and its allure diminishes as soon as the goal is achieved.

A true purpose, however, involves a deeper, more emotional "why" behind the goal. For instance, if you need the car for your family because your current vehicle is too small, the purpose is more profound. This deeper need drives your determination, making it less likely that you'll give up, even when faced with obstacles. When the reason behind your goal is significant and impacts your loved ones, it becomes a source of enduring motivation.

Conversely, if the car is simply a personal indulgence, the motivation might not be as strong. When difficulties arise, it's easier to dismiss the goal with thoughts like, "I don't really need it that badly." Without a compelling reason, it's simpler to abandon the pursuit.

When your purpose extends beyond personal gain—to serving your family, community, society, or humanity—it transforms into a lifelong mission that imbues your life with meaning. The fulfillment derived from contributing to the well-being of others often surpasses the satisfaction of self-serving achievements. Once you have a family or a child, you'll likely find a profound sense of purpose in serving others, which provides a deeper, more lasting fulfillment than any material possession.

Integrate Purpose with Responsibilities: How often do we settle for financial comfort at the expense of our dreams and true purpose in life? It's a common scenario: someone lands a job that offers a salary far beyond what they ever anticipated or imagined. Initially, the increased income feels like a significant achievement, but over time, this newfound financial stability can become a trap. Instead of pursuing their original passions or aspirations, they find themselves focused on maintaining their current lifestyle and holding onto what they have.

In the process, they may abandon the dreams and goals that once motivated them, losing sight of their deeper purpose. If only they could see where their choices would lead them in five years, they might realize that continuing to chase their true passions is worth far more than temporary financial gains. By staying true to their purpose and following their passions, they could find a sense of fulfillment and meaning that money alone cannot provide.

It's especially challenging when you have dependents and responsibilities to provide for your family. The pressure to ensure their well-being can make the idea of pursuing your passions seem impractical or even irresponsible. However, it's important to remember that there is always time for the things that truly matter in your life; you just need to become adept at priority management, not just time management. Balancing responsibilities with pursuing your passions requires thoughtful planning and prioritization, but it's not impossible. By aligning your goals with your values and managing your priorities effectively, you can find a way to integrate both financial stability and personal fulfillment into your life.

Your Purpose May Find You First: Often, we don't actively seek out our purpose; instead, it finds us first in various forms—through personal tragedy, serious illness, a profound spiritual calling, or unexpected events. Though these experiences can be challenging, they often set us on a path that can transform not only our own lives but also the lives of many others.

As a reader of this book, you might feel that God has guided you to your current path. You may see your involvement in your passions not just as a career choice but as a divine calling with the potential to profoundly impact your family for generations. If this resonates with you, it could be a sign that you have discovered your true purpose.

When you feel a deep sense of divine direction or an overwhelming conviction that your current path is meant to effect meaningful change, you may have discovered your genuine purpose. Embracing this belief can bring clarity and motivation, allowing you to pursue your goals with renewed passion and commitment, knowing that your actions have the potential to create a lasting and significant impact.

PILLAR 5: Challenges to Finding Your Purpose

"The pursuit of purpose is an adventure; challenges are the map guiding you to its discovery."

- Anonymous

ear: People often spend hours planning vacations because they feel confident about their success. However, when it comes to planning their lives, the fear of **failure** can be overwhelming. They might believe that finding their purpose is a futile effort or that they won't achieve it anyway. This lack of self-belief and confidence leads them to avoid planning altogether. Many people prefer to remain in a state of uncertainty, avoiding the need to confront the possibility that their lives might not be on the right track. They maintain a "mystical fog" around their situation, avoiding clarity about where their life is headed. This fog prevents them from recognizing whether their life is off course or deteriorating, allowing them to remain temporarily comfortable in denial rather than face potential shortcomings.

Additionally, the fear of **making the wrong choice** can be paralyzing. The decision to pursue a new path or goal involves uncertainty and risk, and many worry about choosing the wrong direction. This fear can lead to indecision and inaction, as individuals become immobilized by the possibility of error. The thought of making a mistake and facing potential regrets can be so daunting that it stops them from making any choice at all. As a result, they remain stuck in their current situation, avoiding the possibility of growth or change due to the fear of selecting a path that might not yield the desired outcome.

Ignoring the need for planning can lead to profound regret later in life. Before you know it, you might find yourself in your 50s or 60s, reflecting on how quickly time has passed and wondering, "What the hell happened to my life?" Many people in that age group express this sentiment, realizing how swiftly the years have gone by. It's crucial to break through this fog of uncertainty and take the risk of making decisions, even if it means facing the possibility of choosing wrong. With focused effort and a determined mindset, you can make meaningful changes in your life, no matter where you are on your journey.

Pressure to Conform: Societal and cultural norms often exert significant pressure to conform to established expectations and roles, which can hinder individuals from exploring their true passions and purposes. Comments like, "Do you think you're better than us?" or "Here he goes, dreaming again" reflect the skepticism that can stifle personal growth. You might hear, "You're having a mid-life crisis; you'll get over it. Just stick to what you've been doing and don't rock the boat." The pressure to avoid risks and stick to familiar routines can be overwhelming, especially as you get older. For many men & women who are married with children, a sense of being stuck can arise after years of feeling unfulfilled. They may feel trapped by their commitments to their families, unsure of how to pursue a new passion or purpose without disrupting their established lives.

Despite these pressures, it's essential to recognize that there is always a way to balance both responsibilities and personal fulfillment. Settling for a life that doesn't align with your true purpose is not the only option. When confronted with questions like, "Why are you doing this? Why can't you just settle?" your response should emphasize that pursuing your purpose is not solely for your own benefit. Explain that achieving your purpose will also positively impact your family and others around you. It's about creating a meaningful and fulfilling life that contributes to the well-being of those you care about. By navigating these challenges and maintaining your commitment to finding and living your purpose, you can find a path that honors both your responsibilities and your aspirations.

No Time: The relentless demands of daily life can often make it challenging to prioritize self-discovery and reflection, leaving little time to explore one's purpose. It's important not to be naïve about the assumption that we will naturally remain healthy and secure throughout our lives. The truth is, none of us have a guarantee of what lies ahead as we age. For example, my father was diagnosed with a brain disease in the final years of his life, my mother passed away just three months after being diagnosed with a brain tumor, and my wife faced a battle with breast cancer in 2021—thankfully, she made a full recovery after treatment and surgery. Tragically, my 21-year-old nephew died suddenly after a routine workout, and a close friend's 37-year-old son went to bed one night and never woke up.

These experiences underscore the reality that life and health are unpredictable. We often take life seriously only when faced with such unforeseen events affecting those we know and love. While we may strive to organize and plan our lives meticulously, unexpected events can still upend everything. However, if we fail to plan and pursue our purpose, we're essentially setting ourselves up for potential regrets and missed opportunities. Effective planning allows us to navigate life's uncertainties with direction and purpose, helping us to pursue our dreams and make meaningful choices. By planning, we increase our chances of achieving our goals and reduce the likelihood of facing continuous disappointments from a lack of foresight.

As you get older, life will feel like it's speeding up—but there is a way to slow it down: **Plan it with intention**.

Flippant Positivity: is characterized by an overly simplistic and excessive optimism that dismisses the complexities of life. People with this attitude often say things like, "Oh, it's going to be okay; your life will turn out just fine, just go with the flow." This kind of mindset can be dangerously misleading, as it downplays the importance of actively engaging in self-discovery and purposeful planning. Such individuals may struggle to grasp the true value of taking deliberate steps to find and pursue one's purpose. Their unwavering positivity often stems from a place of comfort or complacency; they might have settled into their lives and found it easier to maintain a superficial optimism rather than confront deeper issues or challenges. They may not fully appreciate the effort required to explore one's purpose or the significance of making intentional life changes.

In reality, while maintaining a positive outlook is important, it should not replace the need for thoughtful reflection and proactive decision-making. Genuine fulfillment often comes from confronting life's uncertainties head-on and actively working toward meaningful goals, rather than simply floating along with a blind sense of optimism.

PILLAR 6: Passion Leads to Purpose

"Purpose is the reason you journey; passion is the fire that lights your way."

- Unknown

Recently, I came across a mental health video ad encouraging people to seek therapy when they need help. In the ad, a man silently reflects, thinking, 'I want a job that I don't hate. I want to do something that matters, but I don't know what that is. There's something missing in my life, and **I don't know how to find it**.'

For years, I found myself constantly asking the same questions: "What am I supposed to be doing with my life? What is my purpose? Why am I here?" These questions weighed heavily on me, and like many others, I searched for answers that felt elusive. Over time, however, I came to a realization—one that shifted my entire perspective. I now firmly believe that the primary purpose of our lives is to discover and relentlessly pursue our true passions. Only then can we uncover our deeper, life's purpose.

When I talk about passion, I don't mean a single, all-consuming interest or goal. Life is multifaceted, and so are we. We can—and should—experience passion in multiple areas of our lives. You might feel passionate about your career or the business you're building. At the same time, you could be equally passionate about your health, dedicating time and energy to physical well-being. And right alongside those pursuits, you might feel a deep passion for your relationships—the connections you nurture with your children, your spouse, and even your relationship with God.

This variety of passions doesn't dilute the importance of any single one. In fact, it reflects the richness of life itself. We are complex beings, capable of holding multiple truths and passions at once. Balancing these passions is not only possible but necessary to live a fulfilling and meaningful life. Each of these areas—your work, your health, your relationships—feeds into the overall picture of who you are and what you're meant to contribute to the world.

The key lies in embracing all these passions as they come, giving them the attention and energy they deserve. By doing so, you gradually shape a life that feels whole, where purpose isn't something to find once and be done with, but a continual journey that's fueled by every passion you uncover and pursue.

I often wondered—God gave animals instincts. They don't need to discover their purpose; it's built into them from birth. They already know exactly what they're meant to do. But as humans, made in God's image and vastly superior to animals, why don't we automatically know our purpose? The answer lies in the fact that God gave us something different. Instead of handing us our purpose like He did with animals, He gave us two extraordinary gifts: imagination and seeds of passion. Imagination allows us to venture into the future, explore limitless possibilities, and return to the present with newfound clarity. And within each of us, God planted seeds of passion, waiting patiently to be discovered and nurtured.

I believe that within each and every one of us lie dormant seeds of passion, waiting eagerly to germinate. However, like any seed, they require the right environment to grow. These seeds won't spring to life on their own—they need to be nurtured by exposure to the right elements. The key to unlocking this passion lies in our senses. Every time we place ourselves in new environments and engage with different experiences, what we see, hear, touch, feel, taste, and smell can breathe life into these seeds.

It's through this sensory stimulation that a connection is made, similar to the feeling of love at first sight, between a new experience and a dormant seed inside us. When this connection is strong enough, it creates a pathway of energy from the external element to the seed within. The more intense the experience, the stronger this energy becomes, causing the seed to vibrate with life. As it does, the energy spreads throughout our entire being. We may feel this activation in various ways: perhaps it's goosebumps running down our arms, or the quickening of our heartbeat. It might be the sensation of tingling in our forearms, or even tears that begin to well up in our eyes. These are the subtle but unmistakable signs that our passion is awakening.

Pay close attention to what makes you cry, what saddens you, or what triggers anger within you. These emotions, along with moments of joy and excitement, are vital clues to the seeds of passion within you. When something moves you deeply or grips your attention and won't let go, it is trying to signal you to its presence. Don't ignore these feelings. They will guide you toward the purpose you are searching for.

Once you discover your true passion, holding yourself back becomes impossible. You'll find yourself constantly urged from within to pursue it with unwavering commitment. Pay close attention to that inner voice, and go after your passion with all your energy. It's this passion that will guide you down a path leading to the discovery of your life's purpose.

If you're wondering, "What if I have multiple passions? How will that affect my overall purpose?" you'll find that these diverse passions often work in harmony, guiding you towards a unified purpose. Rather than competing with one another, your passions can converge, helping you uncover a single, significant purpose that ties them all together.

Once you identify your purpose, it becomes the cornerstone of how you contribute to the world. Initially, your journey will foster your own growth and development. The struggles, failures, and relentless efforts will shape you, both mentally and emotionally. It's through your passion and the pursuit of your dreams that you gain the strength to overcome challenges and acquire wisdom.

As you continue to grow and achieve, your contributions will extend beyond yourself. You'll first impact your family, then your community, and potentially even the world, depending on the depth and duration of your pursuit. The magnitude of your dreams will dictate the scale of your contribution. Ultimately, the legacy you leave behind will reflect the passion and purpose you have passionately pursued throughout your life.

People who fail to uncover their true passion often find themselves drifting through life, feeling bored and uninspired. Without a clear passion, finding one's purpose can remain elusive, leading to a life with minimal impact and little to no legacy. When such individuals pass away, their absence might leave little trace, as if they had never truly lived.

In contrast, once you discover your true passion, confidence will naturally follow. Your fervent pursuit will fuel a sense of self-assuredness and purpose. Low confidence often signals that you haven't yet found your passion. So, how do you discover it?

Finding your true passion requires an active and intentional search. Consider delving into aspects of your life that you haven't yet explored. Reflect on the lives of the remarkable people you admire; their achievements resonate with you for a reason. Your own passions may be connected to the qualities and pursuits of those you look up to. By identifying these connections and exploring new interests, you can uncover the passion that will fuel your confidence and drive, guiding you to a fulfilling purpose and a meaningful legacy.

PILLAR 7: Steps to Uncovering Your Purpose

"In every brushstroke, we find the how-to guide for discovering our purpose."

- Vincent van Gogh

This chapter is built on the foundation of the Japanese concept *ikigai* (生き甲斐), which translates to "reason for being" or "a reason to live." *Ikigai* represents a deeply personal source of motivation, purpose, and fulfillment. It is often described as the intersection of four key elements: what you love, what the world needs, what you are good at, and what you can be paid for. At its core, *ikigai* helps people find harmony between their passion, talents, and the value they bring to others.

In this framework, we've customized the traditional *ikigai* structure into a more focused approach, emphasizing three essential elements:

1. **What are you good at?** (Your Talent)

   Your talent refers to the unique abilities and skills that set you apart. It's not just about what you've learned, but also about the natural strengths that come easily to you. This might include problem-solving, creativity, or leadership. By honing in on these skills, you can unlock your full potential and contribute meaningfully to any area you choose to pursue.

2. **What do you love to do?** (Your Passion)

Your passion is the work or activities that give you joy, that make you feel alive and energized. Passion is what drives you forward even when faced with challenges. When you align your talents with your passion, you create a powerful force that makes hard work feel worthwhile and exciting. It's this passion that keeps you motivated and engaged.

3. **What problem are you passionate about solving?** (Your Solution)

Finally, *ikigai* is not complete without addressing how your talents and passions can be used to solve real problems. This is the practical aspect of purpose: how can you add value to the world by addressing specific challenges or needs? Finding a solution, you are uniquely suited to provide helps you contribute positively to society while ensuring your work feels meaningful.

By blending these three elements—your talent, passion, and solution—you can build a life of purpose, satisfaction, and impact. This customized approach to *ikigai* simplifies the traditional model, focusing on what truly matters: using your gifts to solve real problems while doing what you love. It's about finding alignment between what you're naturally good at and what the world needs, allowing you to live with a deep sense of fulfillment.

1. What are you good at? (Your Talent)

Let's dive into "Your Talent"—what are you really good at? This might seem straightforward, but people often hesitate to recognize their natural strengths. What feels easy to you might be impressive to others. So, it's important to look deeper to find your hidden talents. Remember, discovering these talents takes time, so **BE PATIENT** with yourself.

Start by thinking about these key questions to help you reflect on your talents:

What are your strengths?
What abilities or traits do you rely on most when facing challenges?

What are you really good at?
Think about tasks or skills that come easily to you, even if they don't seem special.

What do you find easy that others may struggle with?
Your talents often show up in things you do effortlessly, while others might find them hard.

What have you always been recognized for, even from a young age?
Think about the qualities or skills you've been praised for throughout your life.

What do people compliment you on?
Feedback from others can show you strengths you
might not fully appreciate. Notice what people admire
about you.

What do people come to you for help with?
If people often ask for your advice or help in a certain
area, it's a sign of a talent you might not fully recognize.

What do you learn or pick up faster than others?
Think about skills or subjects that come naturally to
you, where you excel faster than others.

**What problem do people often ask you to solve
because of your talent or skill?**
Consider situations where your skills stand out. If
people often turn to you for solutions, it's likely because
they see a strength in you.

**What comes so naturally to you that you don't even
realize it's a talent?**
Some talents are so second nature that you might not
even notice them. What do you do easily, almost
without thinking?

If you don't know, ask someone who knows you well.
It's often difficult to see our own abilities clearly because
we're so used to them. Just like you can't read the label
from inside the bottle, it's hard to recognize the unique
qualities that set you apart. Reach out to trusted friends,
family members, or colleagues—people who have seen
you in different situations and can offer valuable insights.
They may notice talents or traits that you overlook

because they come so naturally to you. Asking for their perspective can give you a fresh, objective view of what makes you stand out and help you discover strengths you didn't even realize you had. Their feedback could be the key to unlocking hidden abilities and understanding what truly makes you exceptional.

Consider these sample answers for inspiration

1. "I'm great at meeting tight deadlines and staying organized under pressure."
2. "I can fix just about anything around the house, from leaky faucets to broken furniture."
3. "I'm good at managing people and making sure the team stays on track."
4. "I'm a natural problem solver; I can figure out what's wrong quickly."
5. "I'm known for my attention to detail, especially in my paperwork and reports."
6. "People say I'm great at resolving conflicts and bringing people together."
7. "I can stay calm in emergency situations and make quick decisions."
8. "I'm good at crunching numbers and figuring out complex financials."
9. "I find it easy to multitask, managing several projects at the same time."
10. "I've always been recognized for my ability to lead a team and keep everyone motivated."
11. "I get compliments on my ability to build and repair things."

12. "People often ask me to help with Excel spreadsheets because I'm good at organizing data."
13. "I'm really good at diagnosing car problems and doing basic repairs."
14. "I pick up new computer software quickly and can teach others how to use it."
15. "I'm great at making sure everything runs smoothly in the office."
16. "People come to me for advice on how to handle difficult clients or customers."
17. "I'm good at talking to people and explaining complicated ideas in simple ways."
18. "I'm often the one who can figure out how to fix stuff when it breaks."
19. "I've been praised for my leadership skills in high-pressure environments."
20. "I can type fast and handle high volumes of paperwork without making mistakes."
21. "People say I'm great at public speaking and leading presentations."
22. "I'm known for being able to think on my feet and solve problems on the spot."
23. "I can easily figure out how to handle difficult financial situations at work."
24. "People come to me when they need help fixing their appliances."
25. "I get asked to handle project management because I'm good at organizing everything."
26. "I'm known for my patience and being able to work well under stress."

27. "People come to me for advice on how to improve their resumes and career profiles."
28. "I'm good at graphic design and making creative presentations for work."
29. "I'm known for my mechanical skills and ability to repair almost anything."
30. "People say I'm a fast learner when it comes to new tools and technology."
31. "People ask me to plan events because I'm organized and handle stress well."
32. "People come to me when they need help brainstorming creative ideas."
33. "I've always been recognized for my ability to manage finances and budgets."
34. "I'm good at painting and doing home renovations."
35. "People say I'm great at mentoring younger team members and helping them grow."
36. "I'm good at organizing spaces and making sure everything is in order."
37. "I'm often asked to handle customer service issues because I stay calm under pressure."
38. "People say I'm great at networking and building relationships with clients."
39. "I've always been recognized for my woodworking and craftsmanship."
40. "People come to me when they need negotiating deals because I'm good at it."

Here are more example answers to help you think about your talents:

1. I'm good at video games.
2. I'm good at selling things.
3. I'm good at public speaking.
4. I'm good at bartering and getting good deals.
5. I'm good at drawing.
6. I'm good at painting.
7. I'm good at baking.
8. I'm good at knitting.
9. I'm good at playing the guitar.
10. I'm good at coding.
11. I'm good at designing websites.
12. I'm good at photography.
13. I'm good at video editing
14. I'm good at organizing events.
15. I'm good at writing poetry.
16. I'm good at playing chess.
17. I'm good at making people laugh.
18. I'm good at managing finances.
19. I'm good at planning trips.
20. I'm good at fixing electronics.
21. I'm good at sculpting.
22. I'm good at acting.
23. I'm good at teaching others.
24. I'm good at coaching sports.
25. I'm good at hiking and navigating trails.
26. I'm good at playing an instrument.
27. I'm good at crafting.
28. I'm good at improvisation.
29. I'm good at gardening.

30. I'm good at maintaining cars.
31. I'm good at writing essays.
32. I'm good at sewing.
33. I'm good at mixing drinks.
34. I'm good at handling pets.
35. I'm good at negotiating.
36. I'm good at planning and hosting parties.
37. I'm good at making videos.
38. I'm good at setting up tech equipment.
39. I'm good at making decorations.
40. I'm good at dancing.
41. I'm good at solving puzzles.
42. I'm good at cleaning and organizing spaces.
43. I'm good at fixing bicycles.
44. I'm good at woodworking.
45. I'm good at making and following recipes.
46. I'm good at managing projects.
47. I'm good at understanding body language.
48. I'm good at giving advice.
49. I'm good at baking bread.
50. I'm good at making friends and networking.
51. I'm good at photography editing.
52. I'm good at repairing household appliances.
53. I'm good at metalworking.
54. I'm good at teaching children.
55. I'm good at running a small business.
56. I'm good at social media marketing.
57. I'm good at helping people with computer issues.
58. I'm good at creating digital art.
59. I'm good at AI implementation.
60. I'm good at troubleshooting software problems.

61. I'm good at organizing and leading outdoor adventure trips like camping and hiking.
62. I'm good at training for and participating in marathons and long-distance running events.
63. I'm good at organizing fundraising events for local charities and community causes.
64. I'm good at mentoring and providing guidance to youths
65. I'm good at creating motivational content that encourages and uplifts others.

MY TALENTS ARE:

_____
_____
_____
_____
_____
_____
_____
_____
_____
_____
_____

PEOPLE TELL ME, MY TALENTS ARE:

_____
_____
_____
_____

2. What do you love to do? (Your Passion)

So now, let's delve into uncovering your passion. Finding your true passion often involves a deep exploration of what genuinely excites and motivates you. Just as people sometimes overlook their natural talents, they may also miss recognizing their passions. Discovering what drives you can be a transformative journey, so it's important to approach it with patience and an open mind.

To help you uncover your passion, here are some key questions to reflect on:

1. **What do you love doing?** Think about activities or hobbies that bring you joy, such as volunteering, sports, art, music, public speaking.
2. **Where do you want to go?** Consider the places or experiences you dream of exploring or the adventures you want to embark on.
3. **What activity causes you to lose track of time?** Reflect on activities that completely absorb you, where you lose track of time and feel energized. You never feel hungry or sleepy.
4. **What problem do you want to solve because it makes you angry?** Identify issues or challenges that you're passionate about addressing because they provoke a strong emotional response.
5. **What personal or family experiences have influenced your passions?** Think about illnesses or personal experiences that have shaped your interests and passions.

6. **What would you do for free?** Consider what you'd be willing to do without any financial reward because it genuinely excites you.

7. **What change do you want to see in your life?** Reflect on the aspects of your life you'd like to transform to align more closely with your passions.

8. **What adversities have you overcome?** Think about the challenges you've faced and how they've shaped your interests and passions. What are you passionate about helping others to also avoid or overcome

9. **What new things have you yet to try?** Explore new activities or experiences you haven't yet pursued, which might reveal hidden passions.

10. **What makes you happiest?** Reflect on the moments or activities that bring you the most joy and fulfillment.

11. What topics do you find yourself talking about often?

12. What things do you do that make you feel most like yourself?...

- **Playing Guitar**: "When I play my guitar, I lose myself in the music and feel completely in tune with who I am. It's when I'm strumming and creating melodies that I truly feel myself."

- **Writing Stories**: "Writing stories helps me express my thoughts and emotions. It's a way for me to share my inner world with others, and I feel most like myself when I'm immersed in creating characters and plots."

- **Gardening**: "Tending to my garden makes me feel grounded and connected. The act of nurturing plants and seeing them grow reflects my own growth and calmness, which makes me feel most authentic."
- **Cooking for Loved Ones**: "Cooking meals for my family and friends is when I feel most like myself. It's not just about the food, but the joy of bringing people together and sharing something I love."
- **Volunteering**: "Volunteering at the local shelter makes me feel most like myself. Helping others and making a difference in their lives brings out my true self and gives me a sense of purpose."
- **Watching and Studying Movies:** Analyzing and learning from films helps me gain new perspectives and inspires my own creativity.
- **Spiritual Studies:** Exploring spiritual practices and philosophies helps me connect with my deeper self and find inner peace.
- **Hiking:** Being out in nature and conquering trails makes me feel invigorated and connected to myself.
- **Being a Sports Enthusiast:** Whether I'm playing, following, or analyzing sports, my passion is ignited and I feel energized.

Here are some more thought-provoking questions to help you dig deeper and uncover your true passions:

- What's a bold or wild dream you have, one that might seem impossible, but excites you deeply? - Forget the cost!

- When you're alone, how do you feel about yourself? What are the deeper concerns or desires that surface in those quiet moments?

- What's the ideal career or business you've always wanted, regardless of financial or practical limitations?

- If you had unlimited money and time, what would you devote your life to?

- If you found out you had three months to live, how would you spend your remaining time?

- If you had just died five minutes ago and were looking down at your lifeless body, realizing it's all over—no one can hear you, but you still have all your thoughts and feelings—what would you most regret not doing in your life?

- What subjects or ideas do you stay up late reading or researching, even when you're tired?

- How do you want to be remembered by others? What legacy do you want to leave behind?

- What thoughts or aspirations frequently occupy your mind, those you can't shake or stop thinking about?

- What did you dream about becoming or doing when you were a child—Is that passion still lingering with you?

In the movie Shakespeare in Love, there's a powerful scene where Shakespeare, unable to sleep, says, "I cannot rest. My mind is buzzing like a beehive disturbed. It's as if my thoughts are a blank page, and a whole world is screaming to be written." The urgency in his voice captures **HIS INSATIABLE NEED** to translate his ideas onto paper. **Writing consumed him**, but it was more than just a passion; it was a means to fulfill his true purpose — to entertain, enlighten, and enrich lives by revealing the beauty and darkness of the human experience.

MY PASSIONS ARE:

_____

_____

_____

_____

_____

_____

_____

_____

_____

_____

_____

_____

_____

_____

3. What problem are you passionate about solving? (Your Solution)

Now, let's explore the impact you want to make. Often, finding your purpose starts with identifying a problem you're driven to solve. It could be something that's bothered you for years or a challenge you've recently discovered but can't stop thinking about.

The question is, where do you want to make this difference? In your field, your community, your country, or perhaps even on a global level? Start by considering the issues that ignite your passion and feel meaningful to you. These are the problems that will guide you toward discovering your true purpose.

To help guide you, consider these key questions as you reflect:

I want to help people:

1. Get out of debt.
2. Free themselves from dead-end jobs.
3. Live a better life.
4. Generate more time to do what they want to do.
5. Overcome poverty and generational poverty.
6. Address homelessness.
7. Raise awareness and support for specific illnesses (e.g., Breast Cancer, Brain Tumour).
8. Support the elderly who are alone or sick.
9. Find homes for orphans or children from broken families.

10. Educate kids on motivation, personal growth, and financial literacy.
11. Solve the bullying problem.
12. Feed the hungry.
13. Provide after-school activities to prevent kids from associating with the wrong crowd.
14. Build self-esteem and confidence to combat hopelessness.
15. Address mental health issues and provide support.
16. Ensure access to clean drinking water.
17. Provide access to quality education in underserved areas.
18. Combat enviromental pollution and climate change.
19. Improve access to affordable healthcare.
20. Reduce crime and improve safety in communities.
21. Create job opportunities in economically depressed areas.
22. Combat human trafficking and exploitation.
23. Improve access to technology and digital literacy.
24. Support small businesses and entrepreneurs.
25. Provide support for single parents.
26. Address substance abuse and addiction issues.
27. Improve animal welfare and combat cruelty.
28. Support survivors of domestic violence.
29. Raise awareness about and combat discrimination and inequality.
30. Develop financial literacy and management skills.

31. Support youth development and leadership programs.
32. Provide resources for individuals with disabilities.
33. Address housing affordability and quality.
34. Improve public transportation options.
35. Provide assistance and resources for veterans.
36. Support community-building and civic engagement.
37. Promote sustainable agriculture and food security.
38. Improve disaster response and recovery efforts.
39. Provide resources for personal development and lifelong learning.
40. Support arts and culture initiatives.
41. Address issues related to aging and senior care.
42. Improve workplace safety and employee rights.
43. Promote ethical and fair-trade practices.
44. Enhance recreational opportunities and green spaces.
45. Support mental health and well-being in the workplace.
46. Provide resources for financial planning and retirement.
47. Combat social isolation and foster community connections.
48. Support conflict resolution and peacebuilding efforts.
49. Improve access to affordable childcare.
50. Address issues related to food waste and hunger.
51. Build better relationships within their families
52. Build a higher self-esteem & confidence

53. Become better leaders in their home
54. To balance their work and life
55. With their health and fitness

I want to help businesses:

1. Increase profitability and revenue.
2. Streamline operations and improve efficiency.
3. Develop effective marketing strategies.
4. Expand into new markets and regions.
5. Foster innovation and creativity.
6. Improve customer satisfaction and retention.
7. Strengthen online presence and digital marketing.
8. Enhance team collaboration and communication.
9. Optimize supply chain management.
10. Provide guidance on financial planning and budgeting.
11. Support business growth and scaling strategies.
12. Improve product or service quality.
13. Offer training and development for employees.
14. Enhance brand identity and reputation.
15. Implement effective sales strategies.
16. Navigate regulatory and compliance issues.
17. Develop strategic partnerships and alliances.
18. Improve workplace culture and employee engagement.
19. Assist with technology integration and upgrades.
20. Provide crisis management and recovery solutions.

I want to help the youth with:

1. Career guidance and job readiness skills.
2. Developing strong study and time management habits.
3. Building self-confidence and self-esteem.
4. Providing mentorship and positive role models.
5. Offering financial literacy and money management education.
6. Encouraging healthy lifestyle choices and physical fitness.
7. Teaching effective communication and interpersonal skills.
8. Supporting academic achievement and goal setting.
9. Providing access to extracurricular activities and hobbies.
10. Assisting with college and scholarship applications.
11. Promoting mental health awareness and emotional well-being.
12. Encouraging leadership and entrepreneurship skills.
13. Offering guidance on navigating social pressures and peer influence.
14. Providing safe spaces for expression and creativity.
15. Supporting conflict resolution and problem-solving skills.
16. Teaching digital literacy and responsible technology use.

17. Providing resources for career exploration and internships.
18. Offering support for overcoming academic challenges and learning disabilities.
19. Encouraging community service and civic engagement.
20. Providing access to quality mentorship programs and support networks.
21. Assisting with the transition from school to the workforce.
22. Teaching life skills, such as cooking, budgeting, and home management.
23. Supporting efforts to prevent and address bullying and harassment.
24. Providing opportunities for public speaking and presentation skills.
25. Encouraging resilience and coping strategies for dealing with setbacks.

<u>I am PASSIONATE about solving these PROBLEMS:</u>

_____

_____

_____

_____

_____

_____

_____

_____

_____

Now that you've uncovered your talents, passions, and the problems you're driven to solve, let's consider how they fit into the three intersecting circles of purpose as shown below. If you have a talent that can solve a problem, you'll make money, but if it's not a passion of yours, you may not find fulfillment. On the other hand, if you're passionate and talented at something that doesn't solve a problem or provide value to others, you'll be happy, but it likely won't generate any income. And if you're passionate about solving a problem but lack the talent to do so, it will remain just a wish until you develop the skills. **True purpose is found when your passion solves a problem people are eager to resolve and pay for, and you have the talent to make it happen.**

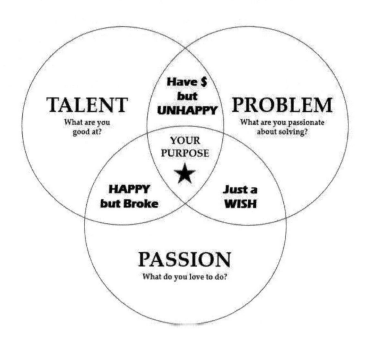

Many people believe that focusing only on your talents is the best way to find your purpose and feel fulfilled in life. They think that once you develop your talents, it will be easier to discover what truly gives your life meaning. While I understand this perspective, I don't agree.

To me, life without passion is like a ship drifting aimlessly without a sail. Passion gives life excitement and direction. When you're passionate about something, you're not just going through the motions—you're energized and motivated to fully engage with it. This energy drives you to learn, grow, and become skilled at what you care about.

Passion helps you stay committed and overcome obstacles. It keeps you motivated to develop your talents and use them to solve important problems. For me, finding my purpose came from matching my passions with my talents. When I pursued what excited me, I found the drive to improve my skills and make a difference.

Without passion, it's hard to maintain the enthusiasm needed to achieve mastery and make a real impact. Passion fuels your commitment and helps you push through challenges, turning your talents into something meaningful. This approach has worked well for me, showing that passion isn't just a nice addition to talent; it's essential for discovering and living your true purpose.

Your Passion is the Gateway to Your Purpose

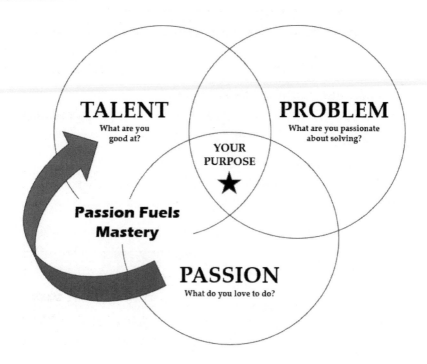

PILLAR 8: Clarifying Purpose Via Journaling & Mentorship

"Embrace the stillness of your mind; purpose speaks in the quiet moments of introspection"

- Mahatma Gandhi

JOURNALING—Discovering your purpose is a journey of growth and self-awareness that takes time and patience. Instead of pausing your entire life to focus solely on this quest, dedicate an hour or so every Sunday to journal about your feelings, thoughts, and what's important to you. Reflect on where you're headed and what you want from life. This process isn't about finding an overnight solution or following a simple formula; it's about gradual discovery, perseverance, and faith.

As you journal, remember that finding your passion, talent, and the problems you're passionate about solving is like piecing together a puzzle. Be patient with yourself and use your journal to capture your evolving thoughts. Write down your worries and concerns to get them out of your mind—putting them on paper can diminish their power over you. Pay attention to those little voices of fear and doubt that may suggest settling for a simple job and being content, or that the journey is too complicated. Acknowledge these doubts, but don't let them deter you. Instead, explore these feelings in your journal, reflect on your aspirations, and remind yourself why you started this journey. Each journal entry is a step forward in unraveling your purpose, whether it's a grand goal like changing the world or a personal one like being a loving parent. Embrace the process of self-discovery and growth, knowing that every insight brings you closer to what truly fulfills you.

My Concerns, Worries, Doubts, Roadblocks:

_____

_____

_____

_____

_____

_____

_____

_____

_____

_____

_____

_____

_____

_____

MENTORSHIP

Discussing your progress or roadblocks with a mentor, counselor, or therapist can be a significant advantage in your journey of finding your purpose through journaling. Unlike yourself, these individuals are not emotionally involved in your concerns, which allows them to offer a more objective perspective. Here's how their involvement can enhance your journaling process and help you discover your purpose:

1. **Objective Insight**: Since they are not emotionally entangled with your situation, mentors, counselors, or therapists can provide unbiased feedback on your journaling entries. They can help you identify patterns or blind spots that you might overlook due to emotional involvement. This objective viewpoint is crucial for recognizing and overcoming obstacles that may not be immediately obvious to you.

2. **Emotional Detachment**: Their ability to remain emotionally detached allows them to address your concerns more rationally and constructively. They can assist you in working through fears and doubts that surface in your journal without being influenced by the same emotional responses that might cloud your judgment.

3. **Guidance and Expertise**: Mentors and therapists bring valuable experience and professional training to the table. They can offer guidance based on their expertise, helping you navigate challenges you encounter in your journaling process and develop effective strategies for addressing roadblocks.

4. **Support and Encouragement**: Even though they're not personally involved, they can provide essential support and encouragement. They can help you stay motivated with your journaling practice, keep you accountable, and offer reassurance during times of doubt or difficulty.

5. **Skill Development**: Working with a mentor or therapist can also aid in developing new skills or techniques for managing stress and making decisions. They can introduce you to tools and methods that enhance your journaling process and help you better understand your thoughts and feelings.

6. **Structured Feedback**: They can assist you in creating a structured plan to approach your journaling goals and challenges. Regular check-ins with them can provide a framework for assessing your progress and refining your strategies as needed.

By engaging with someone who is emotionally detached from your concerns, you gain a fresh perspective and practical advice, which can help you approach your journaling journey with a clearer and more focused mindset. Their guidance can be instrumental in making informed decisions and overcoming obstacles as you work toward discovering your true purpose.

PILLAR 9: Purpose Requires Sacrifice; Close the Doors

"To live with a noble purpose, one must be willing to sacrifice the lesser goals along the way."

- Confucius

PREPARE TO SACRIFICE—You may have 12 different passions, 12 doors you could walk through, but the issue isn't the lack of options—you have plenty. The real challenge is learning to close some of those doors. Some of your interests, while exciting, might be stealing time and energy from your ultimate purpose—the one thing that gives your life true meaning.

To truly fulfill your purpose, you need to focus on taking your passion to the next level. This means becoming a master, an expert, or an authority on something you love. But mastery takes time and dedication. If you spread yourself too thin, chasing too many passions at once, you won't have the focus needed to excel. Instead of becoming an expert, you'll end up being a generalist—knowledgeable in many areas but not mastering any one of them.

Sacrifice doesn't mean giving up on what makes you happy—it's about prioritizing what truly matters. When you choose to close certain doors, you're not abandoning your passions; you're sharpening your focus on the one that aligns most with your purpose. Every great achievement requires some level of sacrifice. By narrowing your focus, you can pour all your energy into perfecting your craft, deepening your expertise, and making a real difference in the area that resonates with you the most.

In the long run, the satisfaction of mastering your chosen path will far outweigh the temporary loss of other pursuits. This kind of commitment is what sets you apart from those who dabble in many things but never fully pursue what they're truly meant for. Mastery requires time, focus, and sacrifice, but it's the only way to truly live out your purpose.

PILLAR 10: Your Purpose is a Gift

"Your gift is not just for you; it is meant to be shared, and in sharing, you fulfill your purpose."

- Unknown

Imagine receiving a beautifully wrapped gift from someone who loves and cherishes you deeply. You don't know what's inside, but just knowing who it's from fills you with excitement. You're confident it's going to be something special, not because of what's in the box, but because of the heart and thoughtfulness behind it. When you ask, "What is it?" they smile and say, "I'm not telling you—it's a surprise! Open it and see." The mystery makes it even more thrilling. You don't need to know what it is beforehand because the excitement is in the unwrapping, the discovery, and the journey.

This same feeling applies when we ask ourselves, "What is my purpose in life?" Just like that gift, our purpose is something precious—handpicked for us by God. It's a surprise, a mystery we're meant to discover along the way. We don't get to know the full details right away, but that's what makes it so exciting. If we knew exactly what it was from the start, we might lose the joy of discovery and growth. The journey toward our purpose is where we find meaning, fulfillment, and understanding.

Think about the wrapping paper, carefully chosen and tied with a ribbon—symbolizing the different

71

experiences, challenges, and opportunities we encounter throughout life. Each of these layers must be unwrapped, one at a time, and with each step forward, we get closer to revealing what's inside. We have to embrace the process of unwrapping, even when it's difficult, because every part of the journey has value. The anticipation, the mystery, and the effort to uncover our purpose are part of what makes it meaningful.

Sometimes, we might be tempted to rush through life, wanting immediate answers to questions like, "Why am I here?" or "What am I supposed to do?" But purpose isn't something handed to us all at once. It unfolds gradually, as we explore different parts of ourselves, try new things, and learn from our experiences. We grow into our purpose. It's not something we discover in a moment but rather over time, through reflection, persistence, and openness to life's surprises.

The excitement comes from knowing that God, in His infinite wisdom, has prepared something beautiful for each of us. It may not look like anyone else's gift, and that's exactly how it's supposed to be. Your purpose is uniquely yours—wrapped and designed in a way that only you can fully appreciate and fulfill. But you have to take the initiative to start unwrapping it.

So, how do you begin to unwrap this gift? It starts with curiosity. Ask questions about what excites you, what challenges you, and what gives you joy. Take steps toward exploring new interests, following the things that light a spark within you. Trust the process, even if the answers don't come all at once. Like unwrapping the layers of a gift, purpose reveals itself over time—piece by piece. But the discovery, the journey, is what makes it so special. It's where you grow, evolve, and come to truly understand yourself.

Remember, the gift is already yours. It's been given to you by God, and it's waiting to be discovered. The only thing left to do is to make time to unwrap it. Don't let the fear of the unknown hold you back. Embrace the mystery, step into the excitement of discovery, and watch as your purpose unfolds, bringing with it the fulfillment and meaning you were always meant to find.

So, go ahead—start unwrapping your gift. Your purpose is waiting to be discovered.

Chapter 11: Strength From Stories

"I'm the only one that can be held accountable for the way my life turns out."

- Colleen Hoover

How committed are you to the dream you say you have? How dedicated are you, really? How much are you willing to sacrifice to make that dream a reality? When things get tough—when the dream seems out of reach and doubt starts creeping in, when hopelessness feels overwhelming—where are you going to find the strength to keep pushing forward? When everything and everyone around you tells you it's not going to work, what will give you the power to fight back against that voice of defeat? How strong is your mind? How strong is your dream?

There will come a time in your life when the dream you've been holding onto won't feel strong enough to carry you through the fear, doubt, or lack of confidence you're facing. There will be moments when no matter how much you want it, the dream just isn't enough on its own to give you the motivation and strength to keep going. And when you reach that point, you must realize that there's a deeper source of power available to you. This power can come from the lives and stories of great people who have walked a similar path. These are individuals who faced enormous challenges, struggles, and setbacks but still managed to achieve their dreams.

Not only did these great people face adversity, but they were also challenged in finding their purpose through their passions. Just like you, they didn't have everything figured out from the start. They had to search, reflect, and often fight through their own doubts to discover why they were put on this path. How they uncovered their purpose—often through hardship and relentless pursuit—serves as a road map for how you can do the same. Their stories are filled with inspiration and hope, offering you guidance for your own journey toward purpose.

Drawing from these great lives gives us more than just encouragement; it gives us the fuel to endure and keep up the fight when things seem impossible. It reminds us that no dream worth having comes without its share of hardship, but those hardships can be overcome. More importantly, though, it helps us discover something even greater than the dream itself—our purpose. The struggles, the fight, the moments when we feel like giving up, are often the very things that reveal our deeper purpose in life.

So, when your dream feels too heavy to carry, when it seems like it's slipping away, remember that you're not alone. You can pull power from those who came before you, who not only conquered their fears but also discovered their purpose through their passion. Their lives can inspire you to find not just the strength to keep going but also the purpose behind your own dream. When you do that, the dream becomes more than just a goal; it becomes the path to your true purpose in life.

I hope the following short stories give you the power they gave me and help you uncover your own purpose. Each of these stories is a testament to the resilience of the human spirit and the undeniable truth that purpose often reveals itself through struggle. These individuals didn't just stumble upon their dreams—they fought for them, sacrificed for them, and discovered their purpose through the trials they faced. Their journeys weren't easy, but they found strength in the challenges, and it was through those challenges that they discovered their true calling.

As you read these stories, let them inspire you to dig deeper into your own life, to reflect on the obstacles you've faced and the passions that keep calling out to you. These are not just stories of success—they are roadmaps for perseverance, courage, and self-discovery. The same power that fueled their dreams and carried them through their darkest moments is available to you. I hope these stories remind you that your purpose is waiting to be uncovered, and with the right mindset and determination, you will find the strength to keep moving forward and embrace the journey toward your own unique purpose.

Chapter 12: Mother Teresa

"What can you do to promote world peace? Go home and love your family."

- Mother Teresa

Mother Teresa was a world-renowned Catholic nun, missionary, and humanitarian. She was awarded the Nobel Peace Prize in 1979 for her tireless work. In 1946, she felt a deep calling from God to leave everything behind and go to Kolkata, India, to help the poorest of the poor. She believed God was telling her, "There are plenty of nuns where you are, to look after the rich, but for My very poor in India, there is no one. These poor children don't know Me, so they don't want Me. But I long to enter their dark, unhappy homes. In your love for Me, they will see Me and want Me. Through your love, they will see Me."

Before she left for India, she set specific goals: nurse the sick in their homes, help the dying make peace with God, establish free schools for children in the slums, visit the poor in hospitals, assist beggars on the streets to lead respectful lives, and set up a home for the disabled, blind, and outcasts, such as lepers.

Mother Teresa knew the price she and her nuns would have to pay to achieve these goals, they would have to venture out into absolute poverty. Whenever she recruited new nuns, she would say, "Whoever desires to be a Missionary of Charity will have to become like the poor, dress like the poor, and live like the poor. We will live our days in the slums and streets, close to the people's hearts, in their very homes; in the dirty and dark holes of the street beggars." She was willing to experience poverty to the same degree as the poorest of the poor, in order for them to trust and accept her aid.

However, once she started her mission, the unexpected happened. Mother Teresa's inner power and strength had always come from her personal relationship with God; she felt His presence and guidance at all times. But now, in Kolkata, every time she prayed, she felt an emptiness inside and could no longer hear or feel God's presence. She felt abandoned by God and experienced extreme loneliness. Where there had once been God's love and light, there was now only darkness and pain. She felt unwanted, unloved, and uncared for by God Himself. Her inner power had vanished—it was unimaginable to her.

She needed to overcome this to achieve her goals. Only with the strength of her mind and unwavering spiritual faith could she turn her inner darkness into her greatest blessing. She internalized Jesus's experience on the cross. Just before His death, Jesus said, "Father, why have You forsaken Me?" In that moment, Jesus implied that His Heavenly Father had actually abandoned Him. Yet, despite His suffering, Jesus's love for His Father was so great that He could never abandon Him. He then followed with, "Father, it is finished. Into Your hands I commit My spirit." Mother Teresa saw in Jesus's love for

His Heavenly Father a demonstration of unfathomable love. No matter the suffering, Jesus would never abandon His Father—and she knew she had to do the same.

She convinced herself and passionately believed that God abandoning her, was His way of preparing her for her mission. God needed to empty her of every bit of herself—her joy and inner peace—before He could use her fully to help the poor. Through her inner suffering, she reached a point of complete identification with the poorest people in Kolkata, feeling their misery, loneliness, and rejection. She knew exactly how they felt—unwanted, unloved, and unclaimed—because she felt the same way. Her heart bonded with theirs; she could never abandon them. This was God's plan; He knew that if she could feel their pain, she would never leave them.

Mother Teresa's **PASSION** was twofold:
1. To follow her faith with absolute devotion and self-sacrifice.
2. To serve and help the poorest of the poor.

Her **PURPOSE** was to bring dignity and love to those suffering and dying on the streets of Kolkata.

So, what power and inspiration can we draw from her life?

1. We are all capable of being agents of change in the world if we choose to act with kindness and love towards others.

2. Her example teaches us to look beyond race, religion, or economic status, and to see the humanity in every person.
3. A life of service and love is a life truly worth living.

These words of hers, are a testament to her greatness:

"If I ever become a saint, I will surely be one of darkness. I will continually be absent from Heaven to light the light of those in darkness on earth."

Chapter 13: Nelson Mandela

"As I walked out the door toward the gate that would lead to my freedom, I knew if I didn't leave my bitterness and hatred behind, I'd still be in prison."

- Nelson Mandela

Nelson Mandela was born in 1918 in South Africa, and like many young men, his first goal was to make his family proud. In 1942, he did just that by becoming a lawyer. Six years later, in 1948, the South African government introduced the system of apartheid, dividing the country into four racial groups: White, Black, Indian, and Coloured (mixed race). Each group was assigned separate residential areas, educational opportunities, jobs, and public services. This system was designed to ensure political and economic power remained with the White minority, enforcing strict laws and punishments to keep the races apart.

One day, a young Black man left his home, not realizing he had forgotten his pass—a crucial document under apartheid laws. When the police stopped him and demanded to see it, he explained that he had simply forgotten it. But they didn't believe him. When he tried to run, they beat him so brutally that he died from his injuries. When Mandela heard the news, he was outraged. He thought, "Nobody cares that this boy was killed. Something has to change." In response to this tragic event, protests erupted across South Africa as people rose up against the pass laws. The demonstrations grew, tensions mounted, and then the unthinkable happened: 69 protesters were gunned down by the police in what became known as the Sharpeville Massacre of 1960. That moment changed Mandela forever. He made a pivotal decision and burned his passbook. That was the day his purpose was born.

The sacrifices Mandela made were immense. He was imprisoned numerous times. His first wife left him and took their children because he was rarely home. Later, he was imprisoned again and separated from his second wife and children for 21 years. During his imprisonment, his 25-year-old son died in a car accident. He begged the prison guards with all the pain a father could feel. "Please, I have to bury my son. I'm his father, it's my duty. He needs me now more than ever." But even in his grief, their answer was cold and unmoving—they refused. His heart shattered, knowing his son would be laid to rest without him.

He was permitted to write only two letters a year, but many of them never even reached his family. He never saw his mother again either—she passed away while he was in prison.

His wife also suffered tremendously—she was jailed for 16 months in solitary confinement and tortured because of her connection to him.

While Mandela was in prison, other anti-apartheid activists continued the struggle, spreading the word globally to "Free Nelson Mandela." And In 1990, after 27 years of imprisonment, he was finally released.

Tragically, his marriage did not survive the long separation—his wife had found another partner—but Mandela held no bitterness. How could he blame her after being absent for so many years?

Four years later, in 1994, apartheid was abolished, and Mandela, at the age of 75, became the first Black president of South Africa. His rise from prisoner to president could only been seen as a miracle.

Now imagine if, on the first day of his incarceration, an angel had appeared to Mandela and said, "I have a message from God, Nelson. Be strong. You will endure imprisonment for many, many years. But when you are finally released, four years later, you will become the first Black president of South Africa."

How long would it have taken for doubt to creep in—after 10 years? 20 years? How would he have felt in the 26th year, feeling like a defeated old man, still behind bars? When would he have started questioning the message, wondering if it had all been an illusion?

So many people experience this same feeling when doubt attacks their passion and purpose, leaving them hopeless. When faced with endless obstacles and hardships, they wonder if they should abandon their dreams, doubting whether their journey was worth it. The vision that once fueled them can begin to fade, and the temptation to give up becomes overwhelming.

But Mandela's story teaches us a powerful lesson: never give up on your purpose if it gives your life meaning. Purpose is not just a fleeting goal; it's a guiding force that drives you, especially when the odds seem insurmountable. No matter how distant success may seem, it is the unwavering belief in that purpose that sustains you. Even in your darkest moments, your purpose can be the spark that reignites your hope, the force that pushes you forward. It may take years—or even decades—but the persistence to stay true to your purpose is what creates the miracles we later call triumphs.

Mandela's **PASSION** was to fight against racial discrimination and inequality.

His **PURPOSE** was to dismantle apartheid and establish a democratic and equal society for all races.

The power and inspiration we draw from Mandela's life are rooted in his forgiveness, compassion, perseverance, and patience. His journey teaches us that great achievements take time. Some people give up after only a few months of effort because they haven't reached their goals, but Mandela's life shows us the importance of endurance.

His own words reflect the depth of his character:

"I have walked a long and lonely road to freedom. I have spent 27 years in jail, and I forgive them. If I can forgive them, so can you."

Chapter 14: Joan of Arc

"Every man and woman gives their life for what they believe. Some believe in little, and so they give their life to little. We have only one life, and we live it as we believe. To surrender who you are and live without belief is worse than dying—even worse than dying young."

- Joan of Arc

In 1412, during the height of the Hundred Years' War, France was largely under English occupation. In the northeastern region, a girl named Joan of Arc was born to a poor family of farmers. Growing up with little formal education, Joan lived the humble life of a peasant.

At the age of 13, she began hearing voices that she believed were sent from God. These voices urged her to take on a mission: to drive the English out of France and restore the rightful French king to the throne. The messages were so powerful and clear that Joan became absolutely certain it was her divine destiny to fulfill this mission. Her purpose had found her.

At the age of 16, Joan traveled 300 miles through enemy territory to confront Charles VII. With unwavering conviction, she declared that she was sent by God and commanded him to give her an army. She insisted that she would drive the English out of France and put the crown on his head as the rightful king of France.

This seemed utterly unbelievable. How could a 16-year-old girl possess the conviction and courage to stand before a future king and demand an army to lead? Despite his advisors warning him not to trust her, Charles VII was conflicted. He feared that if she was telling the truth and he dismissed her, he would be defying God himself. So, he took a calculated risk, granting her a small army to test her claims, eager to see if she truly had divine backing and what would happen next.

She led the army on horseback, dressed in full armor, with her hair cut short to look like a male soldier. She carried a sword and marched under a banner depicting the Virgin Mary holding baby Jesus, supported by two angels. Joan's strength didn't come from any proof of her own abilities—she had none. Her confidence came entirely from her unshakable faith and her deep connection with God. Without that, there's no way she could have accomplished what she did.

After her first victory, Charles VII gave Joan an even larger army to push the English out. At one of the most crucial battles, the French army stood on one side, and thousands of English soldiers faced them on the other. Joan rode alone toward the English soldiers and shouted with unwavering conviction:

"I have a message for your King Henry. It is a message from God. Go home. Go now in peace. If you do not go now, you will be buried in this field. I have seen

enough blood, but if you want more, I can't stop you. I can only warn you — it will be your blood, not ours. I am waiting for your answer."

With tears streaming down her face, she prayed they would turn back.

Then, a miracle happened — the English army turned and left the battlefield. Because of this victory, Joan of Arc, only 17 years old, was able to complete her mission from God and place the crown on Charles VII's head, making him the true King of France.

Two years later, out of revenge, the English captured Joan of Arc and burned her at the stake at just 19 years of age. They accused her of dressing like a man, defying the church's authority, and committing heresy by holding beliefs that clashed with their teachings. But rumors spread that the real reason the English went after Joan was because their soldiers feared she might truly be sent by God — and they had no choice but to dispose of her.

In 1920, the Catholic Church canonized her as a saint, honoring her unwavering faith and steadfast commitment to her divine mission.

Joan of Arc's **PASSION** was to follow her faith, regardless of the consequences she faced.

Her **PURPOSE** was to crown Charles VII as the king of France and to lead the French army to victory during the Hundred Years' War.

So, what power and inspiration can we draw from Joan of Arc's life? We can embrace her unwavering conviction and courage to stand up for our beliefs, staying true to our values even in the face of adversity. As a leader, she ignited a fire in the hearts of those around her, inspiring them to take action. Her charisma and passion turned ordinary individuals into fearless warriors. Let her story remind us that it is our conviction and passion that can light the way for others, encouraging them to follow our lead.

At just 16, she risked everything for her purpose, including her life. How old are you, and what are you risking for yours?

Terry Gogna

Chapter 15: HRH Prince Philip

"If I had my way, we would have a lot more leaders who were more concerned with their purpose and responsibilities than their own popularity."

- HRH Prince Philip

In England, during his 40s, Prince Philip went through a significant midlife crisis. Despite having great wealth and influence, he felt lost and struggled to find purpose in his life. His pride kept him from sharing his feelings with anyone.

As a young man, he had been an adventurer and a pilot in the Royal Navy, enjoying excitement and challenge. But when his wife became queen, he set aside his own dreams and faced the reality of being seen mainly as the queen's husband. In that time, he wrestled with a sense of loss, longing to regain the passion and purpose that once defined him.

Dean Robin Woods, an Anglican priest, invited Prince Philip to a private meeting with religious ministers from various churches. When he arrived, he listened as the ministers spoke about their struggles in life and church work. They shared feelings of defeat and confusion, all grappling with their own midlife crises.

After hearing their concerns, Dean Woods asked Prince Philip for his thoughts. Prince Philip replied, "I've never heard such nonsense. What you all need to do is get off your backsides, get out into the world, and do something. That's why you're feeling lost. There's a need within each person to make a mark. Action is what defines us — action, not suffering. All this sitting around thinking and talking is just a waste of everyone's time."

A few weeks later, Prince Philip called for another meeting with the ministers. This time, he opened up about his own struggles. He admitted that he had lost his faith and was feeling empty and lonely. He had been searching for something to bring meaning back to his life. He shared that he now believes the solution to our problems lies in our heads and hearts, where faith resides.

He told them, "I was mocking you all for what you were trying to achieve here in St. George's House, and now I find myself filled with respect and admiration for you. In my desperation, I come to you and ask for your help."

Prince Philip found a new **PASSION** in painting and writing, which became integral to his life.

His **PURPOSE** evolved into the development of St. George's House, established in 1966 as a center for exploring faith and philosophy. This initiative has continued for over 50 years since he met Dean Robin Woods, fostering meaningful discussions and reflection on important issues.

What inspiration and wisdom can we draw from Prince Philip's life?

1. **It's Never Too Late for New Beginnings**:

   No matter where you are in life, it's never too late to explore new interests and passions. Prince Philip's journey shows us that following your heart can lead to unexpected fulfillment. Embrace what makes you happy, whether it's painting, writing, or any other pursuit that sparks joy in your life. Each new endeavor can bring a renewed sense of purpose and excitement.

2. **The Importance of Seeking Help**:

   Acknowledging that you need support is a sign of strength, not weakness. Just as Prince Philip sought connection and guidance during his struggles, we should not hesitate to reach out for help when facing tough times. Talking to someone—be it a friend, family member, or professional—can provide clarity and comfort. Remember, you don't have to navigate life's challenges alone; seeking help is a vital step toward healing and growth.

By embracing these lessons, we can find the courage to pursue our passions and the wisdom to seek support when needed, enriching our lives and the lives of those around us.

Chapter 16: The Suffragettes

"It is obvious to you that the struggle will be an unequal one, but I shall make it - I shall make it as long as I have an ounce of strength left in me, or any life left in me."

- Emmeline Pankhurst

The suffragettes were a group of women in London, England, fighting for women's rights in the early 1900s. For 50 years, they protested peacefully for equality and the right to vote. But time and again, the government and the press ignored them.

Emmeline Pankhurst, their leader, believed it was time to take stronger action. She called on women to join her in a nationwide campaign of civil disobedience. Their plan was bold—break windows and damage government property so their voices could no longer be silenced. As Pankhurst famously said, "The argument of the broken window pane is the most valuable argument in modern politics." She urged the suffragettes to target what mattered most to those in power, declaring, "There is something that governments care for far more than human life, and that is the security of property, and so it is through property that we shall strike the enemy. Be militant each in your own way. I incite this meeting to rebellion." She also explained, "We are not here because we are lawbreakers; we are here in our efforts to become lawmakers."

Terry Gogna

In the movie *The Suffragettes*, Maud Watts is a fictional character, but she represents the countless real women who took part in this movement. Everything that happened to Maud in the film reflected the true experiences of the many brave women fighting for gender equality.

At just 7 years old, Maud began working part-time in a factory—the same factory where her mother had died due to the terrible working conditions. By age 12, she was working full-time, unable to go to school because her family needed every penny just to survive. The women in the factory worked longer hours than the men, yet earned only half their wages. Fear of losing their jobs kept them quiet, as most were uneducated and desperate for money.

Every day, Maud watched as the boss sexually harassed the young women, threatening to fire them if they didn't comply. She knew exactly what they were going through because she had faced the same abuse herself before she got married. Her husband also worked at the factory, and together they had a young son, about six years old.

Maud's life took a turn when she witnessed women peacefully protesting in the streets, only to be brutally beaten by the police. She watched in horror as officers knocked them to the ground with batons, kicking and beating them as they lay bleeding, then arresting them. It was in that moment, knowing something had to change, that her purpose found her.

When Maud was asked why she wanted to be able to vote, she simply replied, "Because there must be another way of living this life!" She knew the price she would pay by joining the movement—she could be beaten, arrested, thrown in jail, and publicly shamed. Still, she accepted that cost and chose to join the movement.

Her husband was not supportive at all. He felt ashamed of her actions and her involvement with the group. After another protest, the police arrested her and escorted her home, intending to publicly shame her and her husband, hoping she would quit the movement. That night, he angrily told her, "Don't ever shame me like that again."

She replied, "If we had a daughter, what kind of life would she have had?"

He shot back, "Same as yours! You're a mother and a wife, my wife. That's what you're meant to be, that's it!"

His words echoed in her mind, reminding her of what her boss had said a few days earlier: "Do you think anyone listens to a girl like you? Do you think anyone cares? They don't; you're nothing in this world!"

With newfound defiance, she looked at her husband and said, "I'm not just a mother and a wife anymore!" In response, he kicked her out of the house and locked the door.

A few days later, Maud went to another protest and was arrested again, spending six long days in jail. When she finally returned home on her son's birthday, she walked in just as another couple was taking him away. Her husband had legally allowed them to adopt their son, saying he couldn't raise him alone while she was busy protesting or being locked up. At that time, the law gave all the power to fathers, leaving mothers with no say.

Maud's heart shattered as she watched her son being taken from her. She wasn't ready for this; it was a terrible price she had to face. Losing her rights to her own child made her realize how important her fight was. She couldn't give up now. Grabbing her son's hand, with tears streaming down her face, she said to him,

"Repeat after me:
my mother's name is Maud Watts. Say it."
…**"My mother's name is Maud Watts."**
"Don't ever forget that name, because I'll be waiting
for you to find me when you grow up."

With a broken heart, Maud Watts continued her journey. The following words from a book called *Dreams* by Olive Schreiner gave her the strength to keep fighting:

"The woman wanderer goes forth to seek the Land of Freedom. **'How am I to get there?'** Reason answers: **'There is one way, and one only. Down the banks of labour, through the waters of suffering. There is no other.'** The woman, having discarded all to which she formerly clung, cries out: **'For what, do I go to this far land which no one has ever reached? Oh, I am alone! I am utterly alone!'** But soon she hears the sounds of feet, 'a thousand times ten thousand, and they beat this way!' **'They are the feet of those who shall follow you. Lead on.'**

The **PASSION** of the suffragettes was to fight for women's right to vote.

Their **PURPOSE** was to achieve political equality for women in society—because politicians make the laws.

What power and inspiration can we pull from the lives of these great women warriors?

1. **Be determined and persistent in the face of opposition**—It took 25 years from 1903, when the suffragettes began their fight, for them to finally achieve full voting equality in 1928. If you're tired, disappointed, or feel like nothing is changing, remember the suffragettes. They faced endless setbacks and hardships, but they kept going. Even when progress seemed impossible, they never gave up. Keep striving, keep pushing—real change takes time, but it's those who refuse to quit that eventually break through.

2. **Your purpose is worth fighting for, especially when it can improve the lives of future generations**—These women fought relentlessly for political equality, enduring arrests, public shame, and brutal violence. Their struggle reveals one undeniable truth: your purpose is worth every battle, especially when it has the power to shape the future for those who come after you.

Their courage paved the way for change. After over 1,000 British women were imprisoned, the law recognized a mother's rights over her children in 1925. And by 1928, women secured the same voting rights as men. Their fight changed history, proving that perseverance can transform society.

Chapter 17: Andre Aga$
Michael Phelps

had

"Remember this. Hold on to this. This is the only perfection there is, the perfection of helping others. This is the only thing we can do that has any lasting value or meaning. This is why we're here. To make each other feel safe."

- Andre Agassi

Andre Agassi and Michael Phelps are two legendary athletes who reached the highest levels in their sports. Agassi, a tennis icon, won eight Grand Slam titles—a Grand Slam title in tennis means to win one of the four major tournaments: the Australian Open, French Open, Wimbledon, or the U.S. Open. Phelps, the most decorated Olympian of all time, earned an astounding 23 gold medals in swimming. But despite their incredible success, both faced deep personal struggles along the way. Their journeys remind us that even those who achieve greatness can battle unseen challenges.

Andre Agassi, after reaching the top of the tennis world, struggled deeply with depression, drugs, and his personal life. In his autobiography, *Open*, he revealed that after achieving his lifelong goal of winning a Career Grand Slam (which means winning all four of the major tennis tournaments, he felt empty and lost. He wrote, *"I*

completely lost, unsure of what to do next. His downward spiral culminated in being arrested for driving under the influence, which became a wake-up call.

Recognizing he needed help, Phelps checked himself into a mental health clinic and slowly began to recover. He eventually found a new sense of purpose. Phelps created the Michael Phelps Foundation, dedicated to promoting healthy, active lifestyles for children and advocating for mental health awareness, using his platform to inspire others to prioritize mental wellness.

Andre Agassi's original **PASSION** was initially to become the best tennis player in the world, which led him to win eight Grand Slam titles.

Michael Phelps's **PASSION** was to become the best swimmer in the world, which led him to achieve record-breaking success in the sport.

After retiring, Andre Agassi's **PURPOSE** became focused on education and philanthropy. He dedicated himself to helping underprivileged children through the Andre Agassi Foundation for Education, aiming to provide them with better educational opportunities.

Michael Phelps's **PURPOSE** shifted to advocating for mental health awareness and promoting healthy lifestyles for children. Through the Michael Phelps Foundation, he worked to inspire young people to prioritize their physical and mental well-being.

Through the platforms of influence, they had created with their fame and achievements, they were able to refocus themselves on newfound **PURPOSES** that made a meaningful impact on the lives of others.

After retiring, Andre Agassi dedicated himself to education and philanthropy, helping underprivileged children through the Andre Agassi Foundation for Education to provide them with better educational opportunities.

Similarly, Michael Phelps shifted his focus to advocating for mental health awareness and promoting healthy lifestyles for children through the Michael Phelps Foundation, inspiring young people to prioritize their physical and mental well-being.

What power and inspiration can we draw from the lives of these remarkable athletes?

The lesson here is profound: even in our darkest moments, we can discover meaning and purpose. Agassi and Phelps remind us that personal struggles can lead to transformative change—not just for ourselves, but for those around us. Their journeys teach us that true fulfillment often comes from serving others rather than solely chasing medals and accolades. While winning can bring temporary joy, it's the impact we have on others that creates lasting fulfillment.

If they had realized earlier that their achievements, trophies, and superstar status would create a powerful platform for success and influence—enabling them to affect the lives of thousands in the future—they might not have struggled as much after retiring.

Chapter 18: Jessica Watson

"If you truly want to live life, you have to get involved, pursue your passions, and dream big."

- Jessica Watson

Jessica Watson became the youngest person to sail solo around the world at just 16 years old. Her journey toward that incredible feat began when she was only 11. Struggling with dyslexia, Jessica found reading difficult, but her mom would read her adventure stories. One of those stories was about Jesse Martin, a 17-year-old who had sailed around the world alone. That tale lit a spark in Jessica. If he could do it, she thought, why couldn't she?

By the age of 13, she had made up her mind and boldly told her parents she was going to sail around the world. Unsure if they truly believed her, she felt she needed to prove she was serious.

Determined to achieve her goal, Jessica began by gaining experience sailing alongside seasoned sailors, step by step preparing herself for the journey of a lifetime.

She had to master navigation, including how to chart her course by the stars, as well as learn how to repair engines and stitch sails. But the preparation didn't stop there. Jessica also had to develop other vital skills—understanding the right nutrition for an extended voyage and learning first aid, knowing she'd be entirely on her own.

Financially, she faced another challenge. Working as a dishwasher in a restaurant, she realized it would take her until age 40 to afford the kind of voyage she wanted — and by then, she certainly wouldn't break any age records. So, she had to find supporters and sponsors to help raise the necessary funds.

Can you imagine being 14 years old and picking up the phone to fundraise, calling marketing directors at major companies, and asking for their support? It was incredibly difficult, but Jessica started with local backers. Slowly, her support grew, because people couldn't believe what they were hearing — a teenager with such an audacious goal.

Jessica now teaches that 90% of her success came from preparation before the journey. The adventure may be thrilling, but the real work — 90% of it — is in the preparation. Only 10% is the voyage itself.

Risk management was at the top of her list. The boat she received was donated but had to be completely renovated and outfitted with new equipment. Every detail had to be perfect before she could even think about setting sail. Forget the excitement of the adventure; managing risks was key. Every potential situation had to be anticipated, and solutions identified ahead of time.

There were so many people who believed in her dream and worked with her seven days a week, some flying in from across the country, eager to help her succeed.

Her boat was painted pink, and with everything in place, Jessica was ready to take on the world.

Jessica had to do trial runs alone to prepare for her journey. On the very first night of her first trial, after all the preparation and high expectations, disaster struck — she collided with a 63,000-ton container ship, causing significant damage to her boat.

Instead of being discouraged, Jessica used the collision as an opportunity to improve. The incident led to upgrading the equipment on her boat, giving her better awareness of surrounding ships and preventing future collisions. Ironically, that setback gave her more confidence for the journey ahead.

She later said that when she officially started her voyage, she felt more prepared and confident because of that accident. It had tested her under extreme pressure, and she survived. She knew how to handle crises, and that gave her an inner strength she didn't have before.

Jessica proved to herself that she could stay calm and collected under enormous stress. This experience made her ready to face the world, even when everyone around her doubted her chances of success.

Jessica spent 210 days sailing non-stop, solo, around the world. During her journey, she faced one of her most terrifying challenges—a category four cyclone. The storm brought 10-meter waves, and her boat was knocked down four times, completely flipped upside down in the pitch-black darkness. It was a horrifying experience, and she could hardly believe her boat survived the crushing force of the waves.

Despite the terror, what kept her going was the thought of her family. She didn't want to put them through the pain of losing her. That became her driving force—the number one thing that gave her the strength and confidence to push forward, even in the most overwhelming moments.

Amidst the challenges of her solo journey, there were moments of breathtaking beauty that made it all worthwhile. Dolphins would swim alongside her boat, and on some nights, when the wind was still, the ocean became a mirror. The stars above reflected perfectly on the water, creating the illusion that the sky and sea were one.

It was an awe-inspiring experience to witness such beauty alone, with no one else in sight for eight months. She hadn't encountered another human being in all that time and only saw land three or four times—always miles away. These moments of solitude in the vast ocean left a deep impression on her, adding to the wonder and magic of her incredible journey.

When she finally returned home, Jessica was overwhelmed with joy at the vibrant colours of trees, flowers, and land—things she hadn't seen for months. Her family's faces filled her with wonder; she couldn't stop staring at them after eight long months of solitude.

Though people called her a hero, Jessica felt anything but. She saw herself as just an ordinary girl, inspired by another ordinary person who had accomplished a similar feat. After her journey, she wrote a book and began receiving messages from countless individuals whose lives she had touched. One girl shared how, after reading Jessica's story, she found the courage to change schools and join the chess team.

These small yet powerful transformations illustrate the impact of courage. When we step out of our comfort zones and share our experiences, we inspire others to do the same. Everyone has the power to make their dreams come true. While inspiration is abundant, it's crucial to take action and make the decision to pursue those dreams. Living our dreams is far more fulfilling than merely imagining them.

Jessica's **PASSION** was adventure, and sailing was her chosen way to experience it.

Her **PURPOSE** was to prove that if an ordinary boy like Jesse Martin could sail around the world at the age of 17, then an ordinary girl like her could do it too.

What power and inspiration can we pull from Jessica Watson's life?

1. **Preparation is Key**: Jessica's journey teaches us that success is largely about preparation—90% preparation and only 10% the actual voyage. By practicing how to handle potential challenges, she built the confidence needed to face the unpredictable nature of sailing solo.

2. **Fearlessness in Pursuing Dreams**: If a 16-year-old girl could muster the courage to sail alone for eight months, risking her life for an incredible adventure, what excuses do we have for not pursuing our passions? Jessica's determination reminds us that while the path may be daunting, preparation and courage empower us to chase our dreams and embrace our potential without fear.

Terry Gogna

Chapter 19: Malala Yousafzai

"I don't want to be thought of as the "girl who was shot by the Taliban" but the "girl who fought for education." This is the cause to which I want to devote my life."

- Malala Yousafzai

Malala Yousafzai was born in Pakistan in 1997, growing up in a region filled with violence and conflict, especially after the Taliban took control. Despite these dangers, Malala was determined to get an education. At just 11 years old, she bravely spoke out about the importance of girls' education. Tragically, in 2012, when she was 15, she was shot in the head by a Taliban gunman while riding the bus home from school. This horrific attack was meant to silence her and intimidate all girls who dared to advocate for their rights. Malala's courage in the face of such adversity stands as a powerful testament to the fight for education and equality.

After Malala was shot on the bus, she was rushed to a hospital in Pakistan for emergency treatment. However, her injuries were so severe that the doctors there couldn't provide the necessary care to save her life. As a result, she was airlifted to a hospital in the UK, where she received specialized medical attention. Malala remained in critical condition for several days, and doctors were unsure if she would survive. She underwent multiple surgeries to repair damage to her skull and remove the bullet from

110

her head. Despite the seriousness of her injuries, Malala's condition gradually improved, and she was eventually able to speak again. She continued her recovery and rehabilitation in the UK, supported by her family, medical professionals, and supporters from across the globe who rallied around her.

Miraculously, Malala survived the attack and emerged as an even stronger voice for girls' education. Before the shooting, her love for learning drove her, and that passion still burns bright today. She believes education is the key to unlocking potential and that every child, no matter their gender, should have the chance to go to school. After the attack, Malala's determination only grew. She became even more dedicated to standing up for the rights of girls and women everywhere.

Today, Malala is a globally recognized activist for girls' education. She has received numerous awards, including the Nobel Peace Prize, and continues to inspire millions with her bravery and dedication to ensuring education for all. Malala was a girl who was passionate about learning—that was her dream. However, her purpose found her through a life-altering tragedy. Her journey serves as a powerful reminder that one person can make a significant impact, even in the face of tremendous challenges. Malala has become a symbol of courage and resilience, motivating people worldwide to join her in the fight for education. Through the Malala Fund, her non-profit organization, she works tirelessly to empower girls through education and advocate for social change and human rights.

In 2013, Malala delivered a powerful speech at the United Nations headquarters in New York, urging that education should be accessible to all children, no matter their gender. Her heartfelt words earned a standing ovation and significantly raised awareness about the critical issue of girls' education worldwide. Malala's message resonated with many, shining a light on the barriers that girls face and inspiring a global movement for change.

Malala's **PASSION** was a deep love for learning. From a young age, she craved knowledge and recognized the transformative power of education.

Her **PURPOSE** was to advocate for girls' education. She realized that her experience could amplify the voices of countless girls facing similar struggles, motivating her to fight tirelessly for their rights and access to education.

What power and inspiration can we pull from her life? Malala's life teaches us the power of resilience and the importance of standing up for what we believe in, even in the face of immense adversity. Her unwavering dedication shows that one person's voice can spark a global movement for change. She reminds us that our passions can lead us to our true purpose, often in unexpected ways.

Chapter 20: Alan Watts

"Better to have a short life that is full of what you love doing, than a long life spent in a miserable way."

- Alan Watts

Millions of people have been moved by Alan Watts' deeply inspiring speech on passion and purpose, whether they've read, listened to, or watched his captivating delivery. His words have resonated across generations, encouraging individuals to reflect on what truly makes them come alive and to pursue their authentic desires, regardless of societal expectations:

"What do you desire? What makes you itch? What sort of a situation would you like?" Let's suppose I ask you, "What do you want to do with your life?" Often, people respond with practical answers, things they think they should do. They say, "I want to make a lot of money," or "I want to be secure," or "I want to be successful."

But here's the problem: If you pursue something only for the money or security, you'll find that it isn't enough to keep you going. You'll eventually get tired, bored, or disillusioned. So instead of asking what you should do, I ask you: What would you do if money were no object? How would you spend your life if you didn't have to worry about making a living? Forget the money for a minute—what do you truly love to do?

When we answer this question, many of us will say things like, "I'd be a writer," "I'd paint," "I'd explore the world," or "I'd make music." These are things we're passionate about, things that excite us and make us feel alive. But then we often dismiss those passions because we don't see them as practical. We say, "Well, I can't make a living doing that," or "Nobody will pay me for that." So, we abandon our passions and settle for something we think is more "realistic." And what happens? We live lives of quiet desperation.

But here's the truth: If you really love something, you become good at it. If you follow your passion with sincerity and dedication, you'll master it. And when you become truly skilled at something, people will pay you for it. The world will find value in what you have to offer.

So, I say, follow your passion. Do what you love. Don't spend your life doing things that make you miserable just because you think it's what you're supposed to do. Instead, find something that you genuinely enjoy, and pursue it. And don't worry too much about how it will all work out.

If you do what you love, the money, success, or security will follow in ways you can't predict right now. Life has a way of working itself out when you're living authentically. After all, it's better to have a short life full of passion than a long life spent in a miserable routine."

What power and inspiration can we pull from Alan Watts' famous speech?

1. **Aligning with True Passion**

   Watts' message reminds us that life's fulfillment doesn't come from chasing wealth or success defined by others but from pursuing what genuinely excites us. If we spend our lives doing what we love, even without an immediate financial payoff, we unlock personal satisfaction, mastery, and often, unexpected rewards. His idea encourages us to reflect on what we would do if financial concerns were removed from the equation. The inspiration here is to align with your true passion, which gives life depth and meaning, beyond just material gains.

2. **Breaking Free from Society's Expectations**

   The speech also challenges societal norms. Many of us are conditioned to follow a conventional path: get a stable job, work for money, and secure a future. Watts urges us to break away from these expectations. His question, "What makes you itch?" provokes us to look deeper and challenge the mindset that prioritizes practicality over passion. His message is that following a path driven by obligation leads to dissatisfaction. By pulling from his philosophy, we can liberate ourselves from the pressures of living someone else's version of success.

3. **Trusting the Process of Authentic Living**

Watts emphasizes that when we commit to what we love, the world finds value in our work. When we master what we're passionate about, success often follows in ways we can't anticipate. This insight encourages us to trust the process of living authentically, knowing that fulfillment will come. He teaches us not to settle for lives of quiet desperation but instead to embrace the joy and fulfillment that comes from doing what makes us feel alive. Watts inspires us to believe that pursuing passion can lead to a rich, meaningful life—one where happiness and success come naturally.

Chapter 21: Denzel Washington

"Don't just aspire to make a living, aspire to make a difference."

- Denzel Washington

Denzel Washington is known for delivering powerful speeches that emphasize the importance of faith, hard work, and perseverance in finding your passion and purpose. One of his most famous speeches on this topic was given during a commencement address at Dillard University. Here's a summary of Denzel Washington's key messages about passion and purpose:

"Put God first in everything you do."

You've got to have goals. You've got to have dreams. And you've got to have something bigger than yourself driving you forward. But no matter how far you go, or how much you achieve, remember this: you will fall. You will fail at some point. The question is not whether or not you'll fall down—the question is whether you'll get back up.

Dreams without goals are just dreams. And they ultimately fuel disappointment. So have dreams, but more importantly, have goals. Daily goals, weekly goals, monthly goals, and understand that to achieve these goals, you must apply discipline and consistency. You have to work at it every single day.

And while you're working on your goals, understand this: true success is not about money, fame, or material things. It's about making a difference in someone else's life. It's about serving others. You'll never see a U-Haul behind a hearse. I don't care how much money you make; you can't take it with you. But what you can leave behind is a legacy. You can leave a legacy of love, kindness, and positive impact on the world.

"Don't just aspire to make a living. Aspire to make a difference."

When you find what you're passionate about—when you find your purpose—it's not going to be easy. You're going to face obstacles, setbacks, and challenges. But that's when faith comes in. Trust that what's meant for you will not pass you by, and keep pushing forward with everything you've got.

"Ease is a greater threat to progress than hardship. So, keep moving, keep growing, keep learning."

Finally, in everything you do, don't forget to give thanks. When you find your purpose, when you're living out your passion, remember to be grateful. Success is great, but remember where your blessings come from. Put God first, and everything else will fall into place."

Chapter 22: Jim Carrey

"It is better to risk starving to death then surrender. If you give up on your dreams, what's left?"

— Jim Carrey

In 2014, Jim Carrey delivered a moving and inspiring commencement speech at Maharishi University of Management, offering graduates profound life lessons about passion, fear, and authenticity. Drawing from personal experiences, Carrey emphasized the importance of taking risks and following your dreams, even when the future is uncertain.

He began with a personal story about his father, a man with the talent to be a great comedian but who chose a "safe" career as an accountant. When his father unexpectedly lost his job, Carrey learned a hard truth: playing it safe doesn't guarantee security. "I learned many great lessons from my father, not the least of which was that **you can fail at something you don't want. So, you might as well take a chance on doing what you love**." Carrey encouraged the graduates to take this to heart—if failure is a possibility on any path, why not pursue what you're passionate about?

Carrey also spoke about how **fear often disguises itself**

as practicality, leading people to settle for less than they deserve. He urged the graduates to overcome that fear, and trust their intuition, explaining, **"Your job is not to figure out how it will happen for you, but to open the door in your head and let the universe take care of the rest."** According to Carrey, when you let go of doubt and fully commit to your passion, the universe will find a way to support you.

One of the most powerful lessons Carrey shared was the importance of authenticity—being yourself. **"Your need for acceptance can make you invisible in this world.** Don't let anything stand in the way of the light that shines through this form." He warned against letting the fear of judgment hold you back, urging graduates to **resist conforming to others' expectations**. True fulfillment, he said, comes from embracing who you are and letting your light shine.

Carrey concluded his speech with a reminder of what truly matters in life: "The effect you have on others is the most valuable currency there is." He stressed that real success and happiness don't come from fame or material wealth, but from the positive impact you leave on others. Using your talents to uplift and serve those around you, he explained, is where true fulfillment lies.

Jim Carrey's speech was a heartfelt call to action,

encouraging the graduates to take chances, trust the universe, and make a meaningful difference in the world—all while staying true to themselves.

As he reflected on his own journey, he shared, "After a decade of being a professional comedian, I realized the **PURPOSE of my life** had always been to free people from concern."

Chapter 23: Kobe Bryant

"A lot of people say they want to be great, but they're not willing to make the sacrifices necessary to achieve greatness. They have other concerns, whether important or not, and they spread themselves out. That's totally fine. After all, greatness is not for everybody."

- Kobe Bryant

Kobe Bryant's animated short film *Dear Basketball* is more than just a farewell to the game that defined his life—it's a heartfelt reflection on passion, purpose, and dedication. Based on a poem Bryant wrote after announcing his retirement, *Dear Basketball* beautifully illustrates his deep love for the sport and the purpose it gave him from a very young age. In the film, Bryant reminisces about falling in love with basketball at six years old and dedicating his entire life to pursuing greatness. Through the imagery and emotion of the film, Kobe explores not only his relationship with the game but also his broader philosophy on purpose.

For Kobe, purpose was rooted in passion. He believed that to truly live with purpose, you had to be willing to give everything for what you love. In *Dear Basketball*, he talks about playing the game with complete dedication — enduring physical pain, overcoming challenges, and always striving for perfection. This level of commitment wasn't about fame or accolades; it was about honoring the love and passion he had for basketball.

Kobe even described how, as a child, the simple things like the smell of the basketball and the sound of sneakers on the court instantly connected him to his passion. These sensory experiences were reminders of his deep bond with the game, and they fueled his desire to give his absolute best. His view was that when you find something you love, you must give it your all, not because of the rewards it brings, but because it's what fuels you on a deeper level.

Bryant also believed that purpose evolves with time. While *Dear Basketball* is a tribute to his basketball career, it's also an acknowledgment that his purpose had shifted. He realized that, though he was stepping away from the game, his life's meaning didn't end with his playing days. He would carry the lessons of basketball—discipline, perseverance, and passion—into the next chapter of his life. For Kobe, this transition marked the beginning of new opportunities to inspire others, particularly through storytelling and mentoring the next generation.

Ultimately, *Dear Basketball* highlights Kobe Bryant's belief that purpose comes from giving everything to the things that matter most to you. He saw purpose not as a fixed destination but as a journey fueled by passion and hard work.

His life and legacy remind us that when we pursue what we love with our whole heart, we find meaning and fulfillment in both the highs and lows, on and off the court.

Chapter 24: Sun Myung Moon

"I did not know what career I should pursue to accomplish, but I wanted to become a person who could take away the tears that flowed from people's eyes and the sorrow that was in their hearts."

- Sun Myung Moon

T he life of Reverend Sun Myung Moon, born on January 6, 1920, in what is now North Korea, unfolds as an epic journey of passion, purpose, and unwavering commitment, marked by a divine encounter that would shape the destiny of millions.

As a teenager, Moon endured unimaginable heartbreak, losing five of his beloved 13 brothers and sisters to illness in a single year. His heart was filled with deep questions for God: Why was there so much suffering? Why wasn't God intervening? And why weren't the teachings from church offering any real answers? Seeking clarity, Moon devoted himself to intense prayer, crying out to God for understanding.

Then, at just 15 years old (16 in Korean age), while praying alone on a mountain, Moon experienced a life-altering spiritual encounter with the Lord Jesus Christ. Jesus appeared to him with a divine message, telling him He had a mission for him and asking if Moon would accept it. At first, Moon felt totally unworthy and unsure if he could even fulfill such a great task. But knowing that Jesus would be his master and teacher, he eventually accepted it with humility.

Jesus told him that for the next eight years, He would be Moon's teacher, revealing the hidden secrets of the Bible—truths that are written but very difficult to interpret, even by the heads of churches and theologians. These misunderstandings, Jesus explained, were causing painful divisions within the body of Christ and had led to the formation of numerous denominations. To deepen Moon's understanding, Jesus promised to take him to the spirit world, where he would learn about His Heavenly Father's original plan of creation and the process that would be required in order to reverse the fall of humankind. With this profound insight, Moon would begin to accomplish the mission Jesus gave him: to build the Kingdom of God on Earth by unifying the body of Christ, unifying the races, and bringing together all religions as one family under God.

Moon gathered all the secrets he learned from Jesus and His Heavenly Father, as well as his experiences in the spirit world, and made it available as the truth known as **"The Exposition of the Divine Principle."**

Moon quickly realized, after accepting his mission, a daunting truth: to build the Kingdom of God on Earth, the existing kingdom must first be dismantled—both physically and spiritually. He understood that those in power would do everything in their means to destroy him. Like Jesus before him, Moon would encounter rejection, persecution, betrayal, and incarceration. He would endure torture, facing countless attempts to tarnish his name, reputation, and even his life, all aimed at silencing him. The cost of this mission would be overwhelming—not only for him but for his family as well; everyone close to him would become a target in this struggle for a divine purpose.

In his autobiography, "**As a Peace-Loving Global Citizen**," Moon powerfully reveals the heartbreaking realities of his journey while highlighting the profound greatness of his achievements.

Moon's **PASSION** has always been, and continues to be, his unwavering devotion to absolute obedience to the will of Jesus and His Heavenly Father, in every way possible and at any cost.

Moon's **PURPOSE** has always been, and remains, to reveal the true heart of God, His original plan of creation, and to establish the Kingdom of God both on Earth and in Heaven.

From The Author

Congratulations on completing "10 Pillars to Finding Your Purpose." I would love to hear how this book has influenced your personal journey toward discovering your purpose and achieving your goals. Your story could inspire many others, and I look forward to reading your email.

God bless you,

Terry Gogna

terrygogna@gmail.com